It All Starts at
HOME

It All Starts at

HOME

15 Ways to Put Family First

Larry C. Harris, M.D.

with Cecil Murphey

Fleming H. Revell
A Division of Baker Book House Co
Grand Rapids, Michigan 49516

Published by Fleming H. Revell
a division of Baker Book House Company
P.O. Box 6287, Grand Rapids, MI 49516-6287
www.bakerbooks.com

Printed in the United States of America

Library of Congress Cataloging-in-Publication Data
Harris, Larry C. (Larry Coleman), 1950–
    It all starts at home : 15 ways to put family first / Larry C. Harris with
  Cecil Murphey.
        p.   cm.
  ISBN 0-8007-5908-7 (pbk.)
    1. Family—Religious life. I. Murphey, Cecil B. II. Title.
  BV4526.3.H37 2004
  248.4′—dc22   2003020288

This book is dedicated to our parents, Fred and Ruth Harris, who, through balanced perspectives and dependence on God, developed a family that is a living testimony to the power of God.

We also dedicate this book to our brother Fred, who had the privilege of being the first to know the wisdom of our parents and the first to exercise the lessons learned. He was also our first substitute teacher. If he were alive today, we are certain that, as the oldest, he would have initiated the telling of our story.

Larry Coleman Harris
Deborah Memorial Harris
Michael Edward Harris
Mitchell Troy Harris
Mabel Diane Harris
Dyfierd Alexander Harris
Freda Louise Harris
Ruth Elaine Harris

Contents

Acknowledgments

The task of writing this book was motivated by the realization of how important family is. I was amazed how my parents had successfully raised nine children to be productive citizens of our great country. How did they do that? It was a story waiting to be told. Ten years ago I was inspired to tell this story. Far too often too much attention is given to what goes wrong in families. Isn't it past time to focus on what goes right, particularly within the African American family?

I wish to extend my sincere thanks to Dr. Ben Carson, author of *Gifted Hands,* for referring me to a brilliant writer named Cecil Murphey. Mr. Murphey encouraged me to continue this book at times when I had decided the project was doomed. Thanks, Cec, for your help, skills, and faith. I also thank the staff at Baker Book House for their confidence in my story.

I am sincerely grateful for the support and contributions of my mother and all my siblings, Deborah, Michael, Mitchell, Mabel, Dyfierd, Freda, and Ruthie.

Finally, my love and thanks to my wife, Bertie, and to my children, Michelle and Larry Jr., for their love and support.

Foreword

You are in for a very uplifting treat. At a time when many of the family values that made America great are under attack, both overtly and subtly, this book is a breath of fresh air. It is written by Dr. Larry Harris, who was my roommate at Yale for three years, and it accurately depicts the godly principles that can lead to a strong and productive family, as well as a strong and united nation.

It is wonderful, after all, to read the story of a large family raised in the South and see how they achieved success by steadfastly adhering to godly principles and refusing to compromise with the environment.

Unfortunately, today's society is characterized by a mentality of victimization and entitlement that frequently precludes achievement; and a great obstacle to not only success, but also happiness, is the exclusion of God's influence on our lives.

Every life is filled with challenges and opportunities. Yet as the Harris family shows, success only comes to those who recognize the opportunities and overcome the challenges. If the United States is going to resist the downward spiral of other nations that have achieved pinnacle status in the

College roommates Ben Carson (left) and Larry Harris at their graduation from Yale in June 1973.

past, it will require a host of people like you and the Harris family, who know what it stands for—for family and for God, who matters above all else.

Benjamin S. Carson Sr., M.D.,
director of pediatric neurosurgery,
Johns Hopkins Medical Institutions

It Starts
with Parents

When I was growing up, no one would have called us the typical American family. In fact, many would have considered us a lot of nobodies going no place.

When Mom and Dad married, neither had finished high school. They were Black and had nine children. All of us were born in the South before the Civil Rights movement took hold. Anyone would have expected most of us to become school dropouts and some of us to become lifelong welfare recipients.

None of that happened.

Those who knew my father, Fred, or my mother, Ruth, understood the reasons. They may have been uneducated, but that didn't stop them. Dad earned his GED while he was in the army. He also received his bachelor's degree in business—but only after all of us had gone through college. Mom, who had quit school in eleventh grade, went back and graduated from high school. Later she completed a course in business machines at a community college.

Even that doesn't say much about Fred and Ruth Harris. They saw all nine of us through high school and college. I'm a medical doctor, my late brother Fred III became a dentist, and my

Fred and Ruth Harris on their wedding day, Fayetteville, NC, April 13, 1949

sister Deborah earned a doctorate in philosophy. Michael has a master's in business and his twin, Mitchell, has a bachelor of science degree. Mabel holds a master's in education, and Dyfierd received one in international relations. Freda and Ruth have both earned their undergraduate degrees.

Yet this book is about more than a record of academic achievement. Our parents taught us values and life principles that shaped our lives and made us strong and loving people. The best way to test that statement is to look at us between the time we left home and today.

We each have our struggles and temptations, but we've always tried to honor our parents. We know the love of God and believe in the salvation that comes through Jesus Christ. That's part of the foundation of our lives, and because of it we've remained active in church since childhood.

Each of us is a productive member of society. Our professions, although varied, are the kind that focus on helping other people. That's part of the lifestyle Mom and Dad taught us: to help others.

That lifestyle included potent principles, taught in everyday settings, about lifelong commitment to dignity, friendship, faith, and giving. At home we all knew the strong hand of discipline, the tender voice of love, and the wise words of guidance. But our parents did more than teach. They lived who and what they hoped we'd become. We found them an irresistible example.

I'm proud to call myself the son of Fred and Ruth Harris. I'm proud of the name and the legacy I carry.

But I didn't write this book just to pay tribute to two wonderful people whom God endowed with wisdom and common sense. My siblings and I have felt for a long time that our story needed telling so others can discover these principles for growing great kids, and all the fruits that labor will produce. Our parents' example to us can show others how to powerfully shape the lives of children for good.

The book rests on one simple concept: For all of us, the family comes first. If I could write about only one lesson each of us learned, that is it. By being committed, heart and soul, to each other and to God's principles, we are equipped to handle all the good and bad life throws at us. Everything my siblings and I know about personal success, loving relationships, and godly living we learned from Ruth and Fred Harris. They showed us: Our training begins with great parents, and it all starts at home.

Chapter 1

Family Gives You a Past and a Future

Honor your name—it is the most important thing you have.

I had spotted the lunch counter and the row of high stools when we walked into Kresge's that spring morning of 1956. Mom grabbed my shoulder and moved me through the store before I could say anything.

Then, maybe ten minutes later, we headed back toward the lunch counter. No one was sitting on any of the stools, so I raced in front of Mom and my brother Fred and grabbed the first one. Mom and Fred, not noticing me, walked over to the side of the counter and ordered sodas for us.

The stool was the kind that swung around, so I twirled two or three times. "Hey, Fred! Look at me!" I looked at Mom and smiled.

Mom didn't smile back. "Get off there, Larry Harris," she said.

I stared at her, wondering why she didn't want me to sit there. If several people had been around, I wouldn't have grabbed a stool. Our parents had taught us to stand up when adults were present. The lunch counter was empty.

"Why, Mom?" I asked.

The saddest expression swept across her face. I'm sure now the change happened in a fleeting second, but I can't forget the pain that filled her eyes.

I'll also never forget that experience.

I was six years old the day Mom drove Fred and me into the business section of Fayetteville, North Carolina. I don't remember why we went, although I assume we shopped for clothes. Otherwise, she would have bought everything on the army base at Fort Bragg.

Fred, who was a year older, was probably more excited about going than I was. For us to drive all the way into Fayetteville and walk through the large department stores was a great adventure. To make it an even more exciting trip, Mom promised that we could each have a soda before we went home—a real treat for us.

Mom had a list of things to buy, and for maybe two hours we were in and out of stores such as Belk and Sears. I had never seen so many people rushing and walking around. We were a Black family, and I'd been around Whites all my life, but mostly at the army base. That day, however, White people seemed to be everywhere.

Mom bought things in several stores, and then she said, "Just one more place, boys, and you can have that soda I promised."

That's when we walked into Kresge's—long before it became known as Kmart. Mom bought what she wanted. Then I knew what came next: a soft drink. That's when I rushed ahead and grabbed a stool.

"Get down," she repeated and walked right over to me. "You—you just can't sit there," she said.

"I'm behaving."

She grabbed both my arms and pulled me off the stool.

I stared at her, unable to understand.

Mom took a deep breath and said in a low voice, "Those stools are for White people." Then she pulled me close and

18

held me. The hug seemed to last a long time before she released me. "You're just as good as any White man, Larry. It's just the way the laws are."

I don't remember all the words she said after that. She wasn't angry, and her voice remained calm. "The law isn't right, but that's how things are."

"I'm sorry, Mom—"

"You don't have to be sorry. They're the ones who don't know any better. Besides, you didn't understand, but here's something I do want you to remember: Your name is Harris. It's a good name, and that means you are as good as anybody else in the world. Your skin color doesn't matter; what's inside you is what counts. So just think of this. Your name is Harris, and don't you forget that."

I never did forget. Of all the lessons we learned in our home—and we learned many—it became one of the most valuable.

That experience forced me to grasp reality in a way I hadn't before. Maybe Mom and Dad had sheltered us too much. Maybe it was because Dad was a career army man and we didn't see what went on around us. Maybe I had been too young to comprehend the obvious.

I can say this for all nine of the children of Fred and Ruth Harris: We have honored that name. We had our share of temptations like anyone else, but we have held true to what they taught us.

I know that we didn't want to hurt Mom or Dad. If any of us had ever gotten into trouble, we knew that our actions would have disappointed and hurt our parents.

When my sister Mabel was in high school, she started to hang out with the wrong crowd. Our folks never told her she couldn't have them as friends, but they made her aware of the consequences. "You go with them," Dad said, "and you become like them."

"You'll compromise your principles," Mom said. "You won't lift up your friends, honey. They'll drag you down."

"Mom, they just want to have fun," Mabel protested.

Mom knew what some of them meant by "fun," and such things weren't acceptable in our home. "I don't care if the president's daughter does something that's wrong—you don't do it. You don't do it because you are a Harris."

A few days later, Mabel decided to leave the group. "Mom was right," she said later, "and deep inside I knew I was going the wrong way. Maybe I just needed her to tell me."

All of us grew up feeling that we had a name to honor and a way of life to uphold. We were proud to be called Harris. We didn't ever want to do anything that would dishonor our family.

"Knowing I had a name to live up to gave me determination," my sister Freda said. "I worked hard, believing the Harris name would pull me through any situation. When I felt tempted to do less than my best, I'd hear Mom's voice saying, 'Always remember that your name is Harris.' That's all it took. I worked even harder."

Our parents were strict; not mean or harsh, just strict. They tried to see what was best for us, not just easy for them.

Of course, not everyone agreed with the way our parents raised us.

"You're just too demanding on those kids of yours," a neighbor said to my mother. That woman couldn't understand why our parents wouldn't let us roam around the neighborhood after dark. "You keep that up and your children will grow to hate you."

"We're not running a popularity contest," Mom said. "We're trying to teach them to do right. They may not always like the way we do things, but they'll know when they've done wrong."

I have remembered those words. So have all of us.

My brother Dyfierd talks about Mom's insistence on our behavior. "She made us believe in the importance of being a Harris. She would say, 'Look people in the eye; hold your head up; be proud. You are a Harris.'"

Dyfierd also applies the concept of family to those directly involved with him in military action.

I have grown to realize that Mom taught us something critical in this lesson about family that has helped me immeasurably in my military career. She pushed us to stand proud and always to carry our heads high. Regardless of her illnesses and lonely times without her husband, Mom knew she was part of something bigger than herself.

Today, when I am faced with a difficult situation, I draw on that inner strength I learned at home. I look at people or the challenge and say to myself, I am a Harris. I am Mrs. Harris's son. It may sound odd, but it works for me, because Mom gave me something to believe in that was bigger than all of us.

I've often used this same strategy to get soldiers to push through difficulty, because what we are charged to do is bigger than us all. Failure is not an option, and we stand firm for our military family.

For example, I was in Bosnia commanding a battalion task force with eighteen AH-64s (Apache attack helicopters) and fourteen OH-58Ds (reconnaissance/attack helicopters). One night in 1999, the Serbian military shot down an F-117 (a stealth jet bomber). The pilot had ejected and was on the ground inside Serbia. The battle captain awakened me and briefed me on the situation. He told me he had already sent in a team. If it failed, four of our AH-64s would escort two search-and-rescue helicopters into Serbia to attempt a rescue. We had no additional information.

We committed our AH-64s to the mission. "You are option two," he said. "If option one fails, you go in next."

Although concerned with the lack of information, my thoughts focused on the pilot behind enemy lines. *He's part of our family,* I thought. *We have to get him out.*

One of my aviators, who stood by and planned to go on the rescue mission, wondered aloud if we could be successful in rescuing the pilot without more information.

I looked him in the eyes and said calmly, "We have an American pilot down in enemy territory. It would be great to have more details, but we don't. Nonetheless, he is family. If the battle captain calls, we are going to try to get him."

He stared at me, slightly shocked, and then I added, "If you were the one out there, I would do the same for you."

We didn't have to go after the downed pilot, because the first team found him and brought him back. Nonetheless, everyone in my unit understood that we were a military family. We would sacrifice for each other.

Because he remembers who he is, Dyfierd holds family in high esteem, as do each of us.

I'm proud to be a member of our family and proud of my heritage of being a Harris.

Of all the lessons we learned as children growing up, the first was that we must never do anything to dishonor our family's name. This meant more than keeping up appearances—this was the principle we lived by. "A good name is rather to be chosen than great riches" (Prov. 22:1).

"They can say whatever they want about you, but if you know those things aren't true, it doesn't matter," Mom said. "You know the truth and so does God. That's all that counts."

Deborah likes to say it this way: "Protect your name because when it's gone, you are gone."

The name of Harris helped us face many harsh realities with strength, dignity, and empathy. That lesson started at home.

Chapter 2

Family Impresses
an Example

*When you live what you teach,
your family has no trouble following.*

D a-du! Da-du!" I yelled as I ran toward the front door, followed by Fred and baby Deborah.

When I was four or five, rushing out to meet my father was the big event of the day. He was then stationed at the army base at Fort Bragg, North Carolina. All three of us reached the driveway before he parked his 1951 Buick.

We had advance notice of his coming, and it became a game. We didn't understand how it worked, but we actually heard his car, through resonance in our TV set, several hundred feet before we spotted the vehicle pulling into our driveway. That was the special moment—we all dashed to greet him.

Still wearing his sergeant's uniform, Dad got out of the car. Solid and stocky, he wasn't a tall man—although he seemed huge to us then.

"Fred! Larry! Deborah!" He always bent down and waited for all three of us to reach his side. He picked us up together and hugged us. Sometimes he danced around a few steps or threw one of us up in the air. When Dad played with us, I felt glad to have him home. In those moments, I realized our house wasn't just a place for our father to come at the end of the day; it was where he came just to be with us. Maybe every young kid thinks this way, but I was convinced that Da-du was the strongest man and most loving father in the world.

"You been good children today?" was the first daily question.

"Yes, sir," we said, but only if it was true.

"I was bad today, Da-du," I had to say more than once.

"My son? Bad?" He stood me on my feet, held me at arm's length with both hands on my shoulders, and stared unbelievingly into my face. "You were bad? I can hardly believe my son wouldn't be a good boy."

"I won't be bad anymore. I promise." I meant that, even though five days later I might have to go through the same thing. It hurt me to tell him I had done something wrong. Even at that age, I felt he assumed I'd be good, and my confession disappointed him.

I always told him what I'd done. Sometimes I had tears in my eyes, but I didn't try to lie to him. He'd find out anyway from Mom or Fred.

Dad listened when I confessed. "Let's drive on, son," he always answered. That was his way of saying, "Everything is all right. Let's forget what happened and go on." Then came the best part. Dad hugged me again; then I knew everything was fine.

I don't remember any lessons pushed on us about honoring or loving our father. We didn't need them. Each of us loved him, and the best treat was to get his approval.

Once Dad had hugged us and asked about our day, he usually opened the rear car door and took out a load of fatigue uniforms. "Give me a hand, boys," he said to Fred and me. He could have done everything by himself, of course, but he asked for our help. That was one of the ways—we realized when we were older—that he made us grasp the value of working together.

He brought home the uniforms frequently. He didn't do it every night, of course, but often enough that we came to expect it. Dad was a platoon sergeant, and he earned extra money by sewing chevrons on his troops' fatigues. If I remember correctly, the post laundry charged fifty cents each, and he did the job for twenty-five.

"You sure got lots and lots this time," I recall saying.

"We'll get them all done tonight," he said. "You know why? I have some good helpers."

I don't remember that any of us did anything to help beyond carrying in the uniforms, but we felt as if we were part of the enterprise. My mother didn't sew, but she organized everything so that Dad had only to sit down and go to work. On those occasions when he got more than he could handle in one evening, Mom asked one of her sisters to come by and help him sew.

Sewing chevrons doesn't sound like a prestigious job. As I think about it, I wonder if some people looked down on my father for doing that. After all, he was the platoon sergeant, yet in effect, he was working for soldiers with lower rank. That fact never bothered Dad—ever. He also cut hair, drove cabs, and worked for a bowling alley on base or as a bouncer for the local Veterans of Foreign Wars club. No honest work was beneath him, because he did anything that would bring him extra income. In fact, Dad always held more than one job. He never complained about how hard he worked, and Mom certainly didn't grumble because he worked so many hours.

Of all his part-time jobs, however, most of all I remember the sewing. After I started school, I often came home to find so many military uniforms in the house that we had little room to play. Just seeing them there was one of the best examples I know of a lesson in hard work.

I can close my eyes and hear him say, "Any honest job is good if you do it right." When I was in high school, he once said, "Son, no matter what the task is, we Harrises do the best we can. Nobody does it better than we do."

Our father didn't demand; he only set the standard. As far as he was concerned, if we didn't do our very best, we hadn't done what we were supposed to do.

Once I told my father about a family down the street who had gone on welfare. "We all have bad times, I guess," he said. "But this is one family that won't have to go on welfare. We take care of our own." He was sewing chevrons at the time, and he paused to look up at me. "That's why I do this work." He said only those few words before he knotted his thread.

Although I couldn't articulate it then, Dad's working all the extra jobs was his way of living the lesson: Giving our best was what counted.

Because Dad put our family first, he never considered anything too lowly or demeaning. Extra work meant he could provide better for the family. Sewing chevrons, standing duty for someone, or driving a taxi—the kind of job didn't matter.

My father had already set the example; it wasn't hard for me to follow. I'm proud of my father, and I'm proud to be part of his family. He made me proud, even when I faced reprimands. For example, I remember an incident (or perhaps Mom reminded me of it) from when I was two. My father had enlisted in the U.S. Army at age eighteen and became a career soldier. He and Mom started the family in the post–World War II years and before the Vietnam Conflict. My older brother Fred III (named after Dad and

Dad's father) was born November 22, 1949. Ruthie, the baby, was born July 20, 1965. Seven more babies (myself included) entered the Harris family during those intervening years.

I don't remember much about the first few years, except when Dad was stationed at Fort Campbell, Kentucky. One day I chipped off a tiny piece of plaster from the wall and ate it.

I liked it. In fact, I started to crave plaster.

When kids get cravings for things such as clay, dirt, or starch, it is called the Pica syndrome. In those days, plaster probably contained lead paint; if so, it was poisonous and I could have become seriously ill or died from my exposure to it. Then I knew only that I liked the plaster, so I ate as much as I could.

Each time I took a little plaster, the resulting hole was obvious, and Mom spotted it right away. Naturally, she spanked me. "You know you're not supposed to do that," she said. "You know that, don't you?"

"Yes'm," I replied and promised never to do it again. But I did it again. And again. Each time she spanked me.

Then I got smart. I must have been quite young, because I still drank from a bottle. When she left the room, I threw my bottle against the wall. If the plaster didn't break, I threw the bottle again. Mom sometimes came back into the room and I picked up my bottle, hoping she couldn't see the hole near the floor. After she left, I grabbed the plaster and ate it.

Mom said that when they cleared quarters at Fort Campbell, she and Dad had to pay the government for repairs—I had eaten enough to destroy a couple of walls, and they had to replaster the whole room.

31

Here's why I can never forget this story: Even as young as I was and even though I did wrong, my mother cared about me. As self-willed and determined as I was, she never yelled, never told me how terrible I was, never made me feel unloved.

She did make it clear, however, that I had erred and that my bad behavior had cost the family money. Yet she didn't reproach me. She only made it clear that my actions affected not just me but everyone. Even then she believed I wasn't too young to learn.

My parents' efforts to teach us to love and respect God, to love our family, and to work hard are responsible for the success of our family. But not only did they teach us right from wrong, they lived a good example and loved us faithfully, even when we failed.

One of the greatest examples was in the life my parents chose to live. In 1953 Dad requested and received a transfer to Fort Bragg, North Carolina, so we left Kentucky. Once settled in North Carolina, my parents bought their first home in Fayetteville, twelve miles outside of Fort Bragg. Like many people, my parents wanted to own a home, and Dad received a housing allowance to live off base. The house was small, inexpensive, with three bedrooms and one bathroom. We didn't care—we had our own home.

As I think of those times, I realize my parents must have felt a financial strain in buying that house. Yet I never heard them complain about not having enough money or not being able to provide nice things. They accepted life the way it was. They tried to make things better for us, and Mom became an expert economizer.

Mom and Dad worked well together. About once a week, Mom had to go to the base commissary for groceries. We had no bus service in our area and owned only one car. Dad got up extremely early on those mornings and left the house before daylight. Many times when I peeked out the window, I saw Dad in his uniform, walking toward the main road. Often he paused, turned around, and waved. It was dark, and he probably couldn't see me very well, but he still waved. A sense of deep pride filled me, and I remember thinking, *That's my daddy.*

He hitchhiked to work and back again that evening. In those days, a person could easily thumb a ride and not worry about getting mugged or hurt. Besides, Dad wore his uniform, which made it obvious where he was going. Within a mile, another soldier or sometimes a civilian employee picked him up.

We were proud of our father. He may not have been an important man to the army, but he was to us. Dad died in 1993, but he left us with a wonderful legacy, something far more important than money or possessions. Just by being our father, he left us the greatest treasures in life. The major reason is that Dad lived the life he wanted all of us to follow.

Many kids around us either didn't have a father or they had the distant type who was gone a lot or ignored them when he was home. In those homes, the moms then had to nurture for both parents.

Not so in the Harris family. Family was Dad's life, and we understood that. We felt strongly connected to him. He was with us even when he was away. When Dad served in Vietnam, he did something I'll never forget. About once a month, he sent a taped cassette. It contained individual messages to each of us.

"How are you doing in school, Larry?" That was almost always the first question. It made me aware of how important he felt our education was. In fact, it would have been strange for him not to mention our schooling. He didn't just ask about my classes and grades, but he also referred to other things I had said or was involved in.

I particularly remember that he encouraged Fred and me to be the men of the house. Fred was seventeen, and I was a year younger. Dad expected us to do everything we could to help our younger brothers and sisters. Although we were already doing that, his messages made us want to do more.

As soon as his taped messages arrived, we all gathered around and listened. I missed him a lot, and so did the others, but hearing his voice just made him seem closer to us.

We missed him, but we didn't feel alone because Mom was always there. While we were growing up, Mom never worked outside the home. "With all you kids," Dad said, "she needs to be there to take care of you. That's why I work so hard."

Looking back, I'm aware how important that arrangement was, especially when I think about friends and others in school. Many of them went home to empty houses. Their parents both worked, and they had little time for true family events.

It would have been easier on Dad if Mom had gotten a job; he could have worked less. But money was never the major issue in our house. Family was always first, and as part of that, Dad believed that a husband took care of the financial needs. He wasn't against wives working, but he wanted our mother to stay home so she would always be available if we kids needed her.

Even with Dad overseas, we maintained a family connection. These pictures were sent to Dad while he was in Vietnam. Larry, age sixteen, helps baby sister Ruth fly her first kite. Mitchell and Mabel work the kite.

Only later, when baby Ruth was ready to go to day care, did Mom decide to get a job. A friend of hers went to work for Treasure City, a new discount store that moved into Fayetteville. They were hiring, and Mom's friend asked her to go to work with her. My parents talked things over.

I remember Dad listening, and then he said, "If you want to go work, it's okay."

That was 1967, and she decided it was time for her to do just that. Days later she had a job at Treasure City. To my surprise, she liked being away and having a new life. She did that for ten years, but then she found her real niche: She became a teacher's aide. She never told me, but I suspect she missed being around young children.

Mom never had any formal training as a teacher. That fact might have stopped a number of people, but not her. She once said, "I have earned a CRD degree," then laughed and explained, "that stands for Child Rearing Doctorate. I've raised nine good kids. I think I know what I'm doing."

She worked as an aide from 1977 until she had to take a medical retirement in 1984 because of a heart condition. She was then fifty-four years old.

Mom didn't have any problem going to work, but I opposed it. "Ruthie is too young to go to day care," I said. I suppose that was the protective side of me. Mom had never worked, and it just didn't feel right to me. I couldn't think of what life would be like around the house without her always being there. It seemed we were pushing Ruthie out to the care of strangers. "She'll be miserable," I warned Mom, "and she won't have any of us there with her day after day."

Mom held her ground; she was going to work, and Ruthie was going to day care. On that dreaded Monday morning,

I went with Mom to drop Ruthie off. I was seventeen years old, but I cried that day. So did some of my siblings, but I cried the most.

When we reached the day care, my little sister smiled at us and then hurried away. She walked over to where the other children played. She didn't cry or look back at us.

Mom and I stood outside the door and watched. I was waiting for Ruthie to realize we were gone and then really cry. To my surprise, my baby sister started to play. No tears or yelling. Within minutes it was as if she had been visiting that room every day.

"It's okay, isn't it?" I said to Mom.

She smiled. I'm sure she knew it would work out. I was the one who had to be assured. For several days I asked my sister, "How was day care?"

"Fine," she said. Or sometimes she gave a lengthy explanation of the fun she had had with the other children.

Again Mom had acted wisely.

I want to tell you three powerful childhood memories about my father. As much as anything else, they exemplify the kind of man he was—and the kind of parent every child needs.

First, the army transferred Dad to Germany in 1959. While we were there, Fred and I both joined the Cub Scouts. Dad promised that he would take us for a weekend hike. He said, "We'll leave Friday evening and spend the night out there."

That was fine with us, and we got excited about our hike and told our friends. The next day we went back to Dad and said, "Jack wants to know if he can go with us."

"Yes, that will be fine," Dad said.

Then one of Fred's friends asked, and Dad said yes.

By the time we left for the hike, I think we were a total of fifteen boys. Dad realized that was a lot of children for him to chaperone, so he asked for other fathers to help him. Only one said he would.

When Friday came, even that father didn't do the hike. He put some of the equipment in his car, drove us to where we started, and then left. Dad had the responsibility for all fifteen of us.

I was really proud of Dad. Several times our friends said to us, "I wish I had a father like that."

Second, a woman named Frances lived next to us in the housing complex in Germany. She noticed that when Dad came home every evening, he was out with us boys. Sometimes we shot marbles or played basketball, but he always had a few minutes to spend with us.

"I used your husband as a model yesterday," Frances told Mom. "My husband and three other men were sitting around in my house, just drinking beer. I said, 'You want to know how a good father treats his kids? You go out and look at Sergeant Harris.' I made them go to the window, and they saw your husband out there playing basketball with Fred and Larry."

"I thought that was a real compliment," Mom told us, "and it shows us that people watch us, and they know how we live. If we live right, they'll want to be like us."

Third, because Dad was a proud man, he wouldn't ask anyone to do anything for him that he could do for himself.

One Christmas while we lived in Germany, my father's military unit wanted to adopt our family and buy gifts for all of us kids. We were seven children then. My proud father refused, stating that he could take care of his own family.

His attitude upset Mom, and she said, "They were just trying to be nice."

"I understand that, and I appreciate their offer, and I told them so," Dad answered. "However, they are my children, and I'm going to take care of them." That was his motto, and he often said to us, "Whatever you do, you have to pay for it yourself."

"But we could have gotten some free toys," I said.

"If I let someone do something like that for my family, soon I'll let them do more and more. I'm their father and my job is to provide for them. That's what I'm going to do."

He hugged us and said his final word about the Christmas gifts: "I'm going to take care of you." Dad spoke so firmly that Mom said nothing more. None of us did. It was settled, because that's the way he was.

His refusal may have been partly male pride, and we were very disappointed. Looking back, however, I see that Dad's attitude only reinforced one of the things he tried to teach us in words: We provide for our own.

As a kid, I could only think about the toys I wouldn't get that Christmas. Years later, however, I saw the wisdom of Dad's words and example. Everything he and Mom did confirmed the idea that what you do is as important as what you say. That Christmas, it was more vital for Dad to teach us self-reliance and independence than it was for us to have toys. The toys would last a few months; the lesson would last forever.

Chapter 3

Your Earthly Home Teaches You about Your Heavenly One

God is premier, and then the family.

As a teenager I sometimes struggled with theological questions, but I never doubted God's existence or love for me. In fact, I can't remember when I became a Christian, and I see how having God in our lives was and is the most important factor in developing and maintaining a strong family. Putting him first in our hearts helps us understand and appreciate the importance of holding family first—whether our personal family, church family, or military family.

And church family was always important. We went to church to worship God but also to be with people who loved us, taught us, and cared about us. We believed that a loving God was always watching over us, and we felt that loving, caring atmosphere in the churches we attended. I grew up thinking of the church as our other home. We spent a lot of time there, and we loved being with God's people.

As soon as each of us children was six weeks old, we started attending the Seventh-day Adventist church. Mom was very strict about Sabbath observance. Because of that strictness, we learned to treat the Sabbath as a day of rest and not just a day when we didn't do any work. She saw to it that one of the first Bible verses we memorized was the fourth commandment: "Remember the Sabbath day to keep it holy"

(Exod. 20:8). She wasn't being legalistic so that keeping the Sabbath became a virtual law. She simply stressed the purpose of the commandment. "God made it so that we would have one day to rest and to forget about working and the worries that weigh on us during the week."

While Dad wasn't a member of the church for many years (he joined after retiring from the army), and though he had been raised a Baptist (he practiced Sunday Sabbath observance), he never asked any of us to compromise our beliefs to fit his schedule. Our family didn't cook anything on the Sabbath. We ate leftovers, food Mom had prepared the evening before, or food that didn't need cooking. Dad never asked Mom to cook anything for him. If he wanted a hot meal on the Sabbath, he fixed it himself.

During our growing-up years, I think Dad believed in Jesus Christ, but he never talked about his faith to any of us. In fact, he was a quiet man who didn't speak much about his feelings. Because he was in the military, he often had to work on Saturday, but he used to say that going to church was good for us. If Daddy said so, we knew it was right.

In our home, I can't remember when we didn't have prayer together as a family each day before school. Mom had us up early on school days. Before we left, we knelt and prayed. Dad always prayed with us too when he was home. I especially remember that they asked for God's protection over us.

Mom also made us study our Sabbath school lessons every night after supper. And when we walked into our classes, every Harris child knew his or her lesson. Each church morning we recited the Bible verse we had memorized that week—and Mom made sure we were ready.

Bible memorization wasn't just about learning a verse one week and forgetting it by the next. At the end of each quarter, our teachers expected us to stand up in front of everyone and recite all thirteen of our memory verses. I never failed to say all of mine.

I couldn't recite most of those verses the next quarter, but somehow their principles stuck and I learned many of the things that Mom tried to teach in her own way. Eventually I realized the Bible was saying the same things we were learning at home.

When we were small, Mom read the Bible to us, and later she helped us sound out the words. As we got older we were able to read on our own, so that eased things for Mom.

For example, by the time Deborah and the twins reached kindergarten age, Fred and I helped them with their verses. We also taught them their lessons. Sometimes Fred and I couldn't answer the younger children's questions so we turned to Mom. Otherwise, we tutored them. Later, Deborah and the twins tutored the four younger children.

Just attending Sabbath school and worship wasn't the end of our church involvement though. We always remained active in the church. If there was anything that needed doing around the building, the Harris family was glad to take on the task. For instance, when we older kids stood at the mimeograph machine and ran off the church bulletins, the young children were responsible to see that each sheet was folded properly.

Our family also always helped clean up the rooms after special fellowship dinners that followed church services. If the church had midweek functions, everyone in the congregation knew that the Harris family would come in and help, even if we weren't there for the event. We didn't resent doing that. Giving was part of our family lifestyle.

Mom used to say, "It's not enough just to take care of yourself. It counts most when you help somebody else."

Many times she reminded us of God by making simple statements. She didn't preach at us, but I did sense, even as a child, how important her faith was.

"The Lord sees everything we do," she said. "You might fool me, you might fool your daddy, and you might fool the ladies up the street, but you can't fool God. He can see everything."

She never wanted us to be afraid of Jesus, but to think of Christ not only as our Savior, but also as our closest friend. "He's the one who ultimately helps you. Regardless of what you do and where you go, if you get in trouble, if you need a friend, you can talk to the Lord."

I never forgot those words; neither have any of my siblings. We still know who our best friend is.

I remember experiencing some anxiety when our family flew from the United States to Germany. I hadn't been on a plane before, and I kept wondering what we'd do if it fell out of the sky. When I told my mother, she quoted a wonderful verse from the Bible: "The eternal God is your refuge, and underneath are the everlasting arms" (Deut. 33:27 NIV). She explained that God's arms were there to hold us up and nothing could harm us.

Mom was like that. When we worried or had doubts, she found ways to remind us that God not only loved us, but also would take care of us. I still worried just a little. But when the plane had been in the air for maybe an hour, I relaxed—and I always believed her.

It would be difficult not to. She and Dad always stressed the importance of being consistent. Mom used to say, "The three most important things in your life are God first, family second, and then yourself." Recently she echoed that idea:

I think the biggest mistake people make today in raising children is that they don't give them a sense of knowing the Lord. They don't stress the importance of prayer.

I prayed for all of my children before they were born. I used to say, "Lord, just let me have a normal child."

After they were born, I tried to live the best way I knew how, but I also prayed with them and urged them to pray themselves.

As I was raising them I prayed, "Lord, whatever they choose to do in life, let it be something that won't benefit only themselves, but something that will benefit others." I wanted them to help people, no matter what kind of work they did. God has honored those prayers.

Mabel affirms this. "The best gift my mother gave us was to help us know the Lord," she says. "The Lord is the foundation that has gotten us where we are, and when we put the Lord first, everything else falls into place."

Not only did Mom get all of us dressed and ready for church every week, but she also got us there on time, every time. Mother had nine kids to help or supervise, but that didn't matter. Being late was not acceptable.

Once we stepped inside the church, we behaved. Mom sang in the adult choir, and she watched all nine of us the whole time. If we misbehaved, she did not let us get away with it just because we were in public. Sometimes she stared right at me or Freda or whoever wasn't doing right.

47

Once Ruth entered her teens, she was extremely talkative. Mom saw her whispering to several of us. From the choir loft, Mom cleared her throat twice. Usually that was enough to stop the offender. One day, however, Ruth paid no attention. She turned and whispered to someone behind her.

The congregation started to sing a hymn, but that didn't stop Mom from exercising discipline. She left her place in the choir loft and walked down toward us. As soon as Ruth saw her, she stopped talking. That was all it took.

Mom turned around and rejoined the choir. That's the worst experience any of us had with discipline inside the church building.

"I expect you to behave in church and in school the way you do at home," Mom said many times. "You don't go someplace else and act different. My children are always good, well-behaved kids no matter where they are." Besides, she would emphasize, "You can never do wrong by doing what's right."

Eventually, all of us became junior deacons, sang in the children's choir (and later youth choir), and stayed active in the youth activities. That, and the fact that none of us ever rebelled, left the church, or turned from our faith even when in college, speaks well of the training our parents gave us and the support of our church family.

Because the church was a friendly and familiar place, I've never been inactive or away from involvement with other Christians. The week I entered Yale University, I started to attend Mt. Zion Seventh-day Adventist Church in Hamden, Connecticut, a suburb of New Haven. Like Fred before me and the others after me, it never occurred to me not to become part of a church even though I was far from home.

This church had about four hundred members and was about six miles from the Yale campus. At that church I met another Yale student named Ben Carson. Later Ben would become a world-renowned pediatric neurosurgeon and the author of *Gifted Hands*. He was one of my best college friends and has remained a good friend through the years.

Both of us became friends with Aubrey Tompkins, the choir director, who all but adopted both of us. Ben joined the choir. He is musical, but I'm not. Still, Mr. Tompkins became a surrogate parent for both Ben and me. When we first started going to the church, Ben and I rode our bicycles. As soon as the service ended, we rushed out and pedaled back to the campus. We almost never made it before the dining room closed, so we had nothing to eat until the evening meal. Somehow Mr. Tompkins found out we missed lunch on the Sabbath, so he started inviting us to his home.

At first it was just Ben and me from Yale. Later, a female law student at Yale named Sheila Jackson-Lee attended the church. Today Sheila is a member of the U.S. Congress from Texas. The three of us set up something we called SDAY, Seventh-day Adventists at Yale.

Each year the church had a fund-raising campaign to support various humanitarian causes. Ben, Sheila, and I collected money by standing outside the dining halls with signs and a container. We explained to anyone who asked what we were doing. More than just collecting money, we also used that as an opportunity to talk to other students about our faith.

Again my mother's investment in my spiritual life produced fruit. She had taught us God was always there, no matter what our needs were.

In late 1955, for example, two-year-old Mitchell, one of the twins, had asthma and developed double pneumonia. The doctor tried to treat him with penicillin, but he had a severe allergic reaction. The doctors tried other medicines, but nothing helped. They finally told Mom that Mitchell probably wouldn't survive.

In the midst of our pain and worry, an insensitive nurse at the hospital remarked to Mom, "I don't see why you're so upset. You have all those other children at home."

"Yes, but I have only one Mitchell," Mom said.

At home, Michael wouldn't take his normal afternoon nap because his twin brother wasn't there with him. I remember those days as a very sad time.

My mother was then six months pregnant with her seventh child. I vividly recall how she cried and prayed. Whenever the phone rang, our parents stared at each other, and I could see the anxiety in their eyes. To make the situation worse, because of complications with Mom's pregnancy, the doctor wouldn't let her stay more than a few minutes when she visited Mitchell at the hospital.

Finally she said, "He's going to be all right." Was she only trying to comfort us and not allow us to worry? Some might think so, but then when I searched her face, I knew she believed what she said.

Besides, Mom never lied to us. "To tell a lie is the worst thing you can do," she said often. "Even if you do something wrong," she said, "don't lie. If you lie about it, you have to lie about it one more time to get yourself out of trouble."

Yes, because Mom believed, I was able to believe that Mitchell would get well.

Indeed, Mitch did survive, and Mom reminded us again of God's love and protection over us. The thing is Mom was often right. She had her ways of knowing. In fact, she loves to tell about a time when the twins were four years old. Their Sabbath school teacher, Mrs. Dixon, came to Mom after class, shaking her head. "I don't know what was wrong with the twins today, but they were determined to run their mouths. I just kept telling them, 'Mike and Mitchie, you've got to be quiet and listen.' No matter, they wouldn't behave."

"I'll take care of it," Mom said.

As soon as we got home from church, Mom called the twins. "You couldn't shut up today in class, could you? You just kept on running your mouths. Several times Sister Dixon told both of you to stop talking. Did you close your mouths?"

"No, ma'am."

"When we go to church again, the first thing you do is find Sister Dixon and tell her you're sorry. I'm going to know whether you apologize or not."

The following week, they told their teacher they were sorry, and Mrs. Dixon then told Mom. They never misbehaved in class again.

Years later, Mike asked, "Mama, how did you know we cut up in Sister Dixon's class?"

"She told me."

"Oh, that's how." Mitch laughed. At that time the adult department was upstairs and the children's department was directly below. "We thought you had some kind of special eyes in the bottom of your feet."

In recent years, like many other families, ours has experienced a variety of physical problems. In 1998, I had quadruple heart bypass surgery; two years later, Michael had a kidney transplant. Both of us have taken great comfort in knowing that Jesus Christ is there to care for us and to bring comfort. Through the many lessons and examples of strength, courage, and faith that our parents taught us, and because of our belief and trust in God, we are prepared to face whatever God wills for us.

This became clear especially on August 8, 1984. Around noon Mom called: "Can you come over, Larry? I'm not feeling well."

Mom would never have asked me for help unless something was extremely wrong. My wife, Bertie, who is also my office manager, canceled my appointments, and I rushed across town to Mom's house.

When I walked into the house, she was lying in bed—and that was unusual too. Her lips were blue, her face pale, and her breathing pained. I didn't have to examine her. I knew she was having a heart attack.

I helped her into my car and rushed her to emergency at the hospital. She was sent to intensive care and then to Duke Medical Center for cardiac cauterization, while I notified my siblings. Within half an hour, all of them were headed home to Fayetteville. Fred, Mabel, and I still lived in the area, but Ruth and Freda were away in college. Michael was in Indiana, Mitchell in Virginia, Deborah in Chapel Hill working on her Ph.D., and Dyfierd in Germany, a career army officer. As soon as Dyfierd heard, he arranged to take emergency leave so he could fly back to North Carolina the next day.

We gathered at the hospital as a family unit. Together we waited, prayed, and worried. Mom was fifty-four years old. I remember thinking, *My mother isn't supposed to get sick. She's supposed to live forever.* I couldn't imagine losing her.

Finally, her doctor came out and called us together. Before he spoke, I think we sensed we would hear bad news.

"I'm sorry, but the heart attack destroyed most of the left side of her heart." He carefully explained the medical condition so that all my siblings understood.

"What about a transplant?" one of us asked.

He shook his head. "She's not a good candidate for a transplant because of her age and the extent of the damage to her heart." Before leaving, he said softly, "I don't think she will survive."

All of us cried, some louder than others. We hugged, we talked, we consoled each other, but nothing seemed to help. In my entire life, I had never seen Dad cry, but he did that day. We held each other and cried some more.

By the time the staff allowed us to go in to see her, we had calmed down. At least all of us had stopped crying. We made an effort not to show how afraid we were for her. Mom knew us well, and before we could say anything, she said, "Don't you worry." Her voice was cheerful as always. "I've talked to the Lord, and he's not ready for me to go."

It was just that simple. Mom knew she wasn't going to die.

I knew differently. As a physician, I understood the implication of the diagnosis. There was just no way Mom could survive.

Yet by the time her baby boy, Dyfierd, arrived from Germany, Mom was out of danger. Her recovery shocked the cardiologists. Almost two decades later, Mom is alive and doing well—even with a damaged heart.

Mom was doing well, but I began to have health problems. I had type II or adult onset diabetes, and my condition worsened. I developed cataracts. One day I became aware of numbness in my toes. I attributed that to my diabetes.

I kept wondering what was going on. I was one of those people who just never got sick. All through school, from first to twelfth grade, I had missed exactly one day of classes. This can't be happening to me, I kept saying to myself.

But it was happening. The numbness increased. I also became aware of other symptoms that, as a doctor, I couldn't overlook. In 1987, I finally admitted to myself that something was wrong—something more than my diabetes. For instance, I had begun to have occasional headaches. Until then, I had never had more than a dozen headaches in my life. The pain grew more intense, occurred more often, and lasted longer. This went on for about three months. At first, I kept telling myself that the headaches would go away. *They're only temporary.*

They didn't go away. I finally scheduled myself for a complete workup at Duke University Hospital.

On one blood test, my serum prolactin level was elevated to four thousand. Normal is less than twenty. The doctor was alarmed and told me that I probably had a pituitary adenoma (a brain tumor). His words shocked me, and I didn't want to believe what I heard. The results of a CT scan, however, showed that I had a large pituitary tumor that threatened my right carotid artery and optic nerve. Immediately we scheduled neurosurgery.

At that time, Bertie and I had just laid the foundation for our dream home. I decided to stop the building and told my family.

"You don't need to do that," Mom said.

"But what if—"

"Shush, Larry," she said, "you are going to do fine. I know that because I've talked to the Lord."

I believed her; I knew Mom wouldn't lie just to comfort me. If God told her I would recover, I would.

The surgery went well. At the time, I had a solo practice, and I had to get back to work just to pay my bills. About three weeks after surgery I started to see patients again. Some days I felt so tired that I could barely move. Each morning Bertie and I drove the seventy miles to Duke for radiation therapy, and then we came back so I could see patients in the afternoon. My favorite song during that time, and one I sang often to myself, was "I Know It Was the Lord That Saved Me."

God's love and presence kept me steady. And Mom was right: I completely recovered. I have come to see that if faith is your foundation, you can cope with devastation and rebuild afterward.

And my faith started at home.

Chapter 4

Family Sustains You in Tough Times

Stand together and stand up for each other.

When I was a kid, Dad never seemed to be tired. He had a drive and a physical energy that kept him going and going and going. As far back as I can remember, he got up before daylight to go to the army base. When he came home, he never sat around or complained about weariness.

Sometimes Dad and his men had to go on maneuvers in the field, where they engaged in mock combat. Then he usually was gone two weeks, and home was lonely without him.

Maybe that sounds strange with our large family, but it's because Dad and Mom have always been the center. When both of them were there for us, everything seemed to go more smoothly. When Dad was home, I felt especially secure. I suppose we all believed there was nothing too big for him to handle. Of course, that would be tested—often.

In 1959 when Dad received orders to go to Germany, we knew he might be transferred anytime. Fred and I, who were then ten and nine , felt all right about going overseas, and Deborah and the twins were too young to form opinions. So none of us objected or complained, and none of us worried. Mom and Dad made all the difference in that they were happy to go, and they helped us see that an across-the-globe move would be an adventure and a chance to learn more about the world.

The best part was that we'd be able to go together. Maybe that sounds obvious, but that wasn't always the case in the army. In many instances, Mom and the kids stayed in the

United States while Dad went overseas for two or three years.

When Dad first told us about Germany, and before we had a chance to ask, he said, "We're all going. We're a family, we stand together, and we do things together." That kind of value system, even when we were young, left an indelible impression on us: Indeed, the family was first.

When did that impression begin? By the time we left for Germany, we were already a family of seven children. That made us larger than any other family I knew.

Now, I liked having all my brothers and sisters. Maybe it was because I never knew anything else growing up, or maybe it was because our parents made each of us feel important and special. Certainly none of us felt neglected or unloved, and I'm not sure how our parents accomplished that. Seven kids (and later, nine) demand a lot of time, energy, and love. Somehow they pulled it off. All my life I heard them say to each of us, "You are Fred and Ruth Harris's child, and you are somebody."

Overseas we wrestled with that. Though Fred and I had husky builds, we were short. That fact alone brought out bullies almost from the first day we arrived. Several bigger kids laughed at our Southern accents. They teased us about the clothes we wore. It seemed anything could bring on their taunts, which bombarded us with a lot of swear words, something we hadn't heard before. Many times I wanted to hit one of those smart-mouthed kids. I heard words that no child should ever be saying. When I complained about it to Mom, she reminded me that they were only repeating the language they heard in their homes.

"Mama, they called us bad names," I said.

The Harris family grows. Germany, 1960. Left to right: Fred, Michael, Mom, Mitchell, Dyfierd, Mabel, Dad, Larry, Deborah.

"You should hear the way they talked back to their parents," Fred said. "They sassed them and—"

I broke in, "When one of the mothers told her boy to get inside the apartment, he sassed her. He just stood right there and said he would go in when he felt like it, and he was going to stay outside as long as he wanted."

"Yeah, and you know what she said to him?" Fred asked. "She said, 'I'll tell your father when he comes home.' Just that, and she went back into the house."

"Won't do any good for her to tell the daddy," I said. "I've heard that boy talk back to him too."

Mom listened and then hugged us, with Fred under one arm and me under the other. "Just remember this," she said. "Nobody but a parent loves a sassy child."

61

Over the years I heard Mom say that many times, but even at nine years of age, I understood what she meant. She wanted to make sure anyway. She repeated, "Nobody likes sassy kids. Why, even sometimes their own parents probably don't like them. Pretty is as pretty does, and ugly is as ugly does. Those parents are fixing to have a heap of trouble with their children."

"You always like us, don't you?" I asked.

"Of course I do." Mom gave us both a big squeeze. "You're both good boys, and I love you all the time. I like you best, though, when you behave and help each other."

And she said: "My children don't fight. We treat each other nice and we treat everybody else nice too."

My parents had drilled that principle into us, so when we lived in an apartment next to rowdy, mean kids, we didn't have any idea of how to cope. Many times when we were eating dinner, we could hear yelling from across the hall. The first few times it shocked us because nobody shouted like that in our family. But who else was there to play with? Too often trouble started when those kids refused to play, instead calling us names, fighting or chasing us, and beating up on us.

We weren't allowed to defend ourselves. How do you not respond when someone calls you names? When they hit us, how could we not fight back? We learned that to run only made life worse for us; it seemed to make them want to pick on us every chance they got. To yell "Stop doing that!" didn't help either. The bullies had caught on quickly that we wouldn't hit back, and they were encouraged to bully us even more.

One afternoon, Fred and I both came home crying. We weren't badly hurt, but we had been hit and kicked and knocked down, and I was humiliated.

Mom wisely grasped our problem. She made us sit down in front of her. "Children, we're in Rome, so we have to do what the Romans do. Do not start a fight, you understand?" After both of us nodded, she said, "But if somebody starts something, you have the right to defend yourself."

Those were the best words she could have said—in fact, exactly what we wanted to hear. We went back outside, and I dared any kid to get tough with me.

I didn't have to wait long. Were those bullies surprised when Fred and I landed heavy punches on them! Defense though was one thing. Violence was another, and was our family surprised when I began to enjoy fighting. It was like learning a new skill. It felt good to stand up and defend myself. So much so that I began to force opportunities to do so. I'd smart off to some of the kids—"You aren't doing that right"—and just a few sharp words were all I had to say before we were hitting each other. Maybe the adventure of doing something new made it seem like more fun than it really was.

One time I wanted to get on the only swing in the play area. A boy from Kansas, who was about my size, was in the swing, and he stayed on it a long time. I asked if we could take turns.

"When I'm finished," he said. Like a typical child he wouldn't give up that swing.

"Hey, how about giving me a turn?" I yelled after what seemed like an hour.

"Wait until I'm through," he said and kept swinging.

We probably went through that four or five times before I started to get angry. "Give me a turn!"

The boy acted as if I hadn't said a word, so I decided his turn had lasted long enough. I pushed him from the back—not the kind of push to make him go higher, but a hard shove that probably hurt.

"Hey, leave my little brother alone!"

I turned around and saw a tall, heavyset kid, bigger than I was and maybe two years older. "I wasn't doing anything," I said, trying to sound tough. The truth is I was scared.

"You hit him," the older boy said. "I saw you. I'll show you what it feels like." He hit me. Hard. Right on the chin. "Don't you ever touch my brother again," he said, hitting me two more times.

Fred, who had been playing a few feet away, was as big as the boy, but he didn't say or do anything. He just watched, because he knew what I had done to the younger brother.

The blows didn't hurt that much, but that big kid scared me. I didn't try to fight back. Instead, I ran home. Fred followed me. I was crying before I got inside our apartment. Naturally, Mom wanted to know what was wrong. I told her my version. Of course, I omitted that I had started everything.

"Okay, boys," Mom said, "let's get this clear right now. Fred, you're bigger. In this family, the child who is older stands up for the younger. Do you understand that?"

Fred nodded.

"When your brother is in trouble, you come to his rescue. You're older and bigger, and he needs to learn to depend on you and—"

"Mama, Larry started it!"

"I don't care if Larry started it. If he's in trouble, you help him."

For a minute, I thought I was going to get away with it. But not with my mama. She spanked Fred for not coming to my aid. Then she spanked me for starting the fight.

Fred never forgot that lesson. From then on, anytime I was in trouble—even when I started it—Fred was right there. He never let me down.

I remember another incident when a boy was riding his bicycle and I tripped him when he got off. He chased me. As I ran toward the house, I screamed for Fred. My brother raced out and intercepted the boy. In fact, he broke the boy's wrist. The word got around our neighborhood: You don't mess with the Harris boys, because they stick together. Now, I loved having my brother protect me, but it was also a terrible thing—which I didn't realize until later—that not only had I provoked the issue, but an innocent kid suffered because of me.

I wasn't mean, just mischievous, and I liked fighting. Fred jumped in to defend me every time. Eventually that constant intervention stopped my fighting. I got things stirred up and could feel a fight coming. The other kid took a poke at me, and before I had a chance to respond, Fred grabbed the other boy or hit him. That meant I didn't get a chance to fight or to defend myself, and that was why I stirred things up. It just wasn't fun anymore.

This lesson wasn't just for Fred. I realized that I was supposed to stick up for Deborah, who was next after me. It wasn't long before I had to do that.

One afternoon seven-year-old Deborah was playing with a ball all by herself. A boy a little bigger than she was grabbed the ball out of her hand, and then he whacked her.

I saw it happen, and before Deborah could let out a cry, I jumped in and walloped the kid. He dropped the ball and ran home screaming. He didn't bother her again.

Even at nine years of age, I had learned the lesson that would be invaluable to me through the rest of my life: We Harrises stand together.

In Germany parents often came out and got involved in the fights and scuffling. A few times I saw a dad hit another kid. More than once when a kid tried to defend himself, the aggressor's mother yelled at him. Some of those mothers used words my parents wouldn't have tolerated in our home.

After her son started an argument, a woman named Mrs. Pollard stuck her head out the window of her apartment and yelled abusive language at me. I don't remember the details, only that the other boy had seemed determined to fight me. This time I definitely had not started the fight.

Before I could do anything or Fred could intervene, the boy's mother rushed out of their apartment. "Don't you touch my boy! You lay one hand on him and I'll bend you over my knee right here and paddle you!" Then she screamed about all the bad kids in the complex, the trouble all of us caused, and what a bad influence everyone was on her son.

Mrs. Pollard scared me. I don't know if she would have spanked me or not, but I didn't stay around to find out. Fred and I had never seen anything like that before, so we ran home.

Like any two young kids, we rushed up to our mother and told her what had happened. She looked out the window. The abusive mother had taken the boy's hand and was leading him inside their apartment.

"That's over, so we can forget about that incident," Mama said. "But if it ever happens again, you call me. I don't care whose fault it is or what the problem is. If any parent comes out there and starts cussing like Mrs. Pollard did or tries to hurt you, you come inside and get me! Don't be disrespectful. Don't fight. Just come right here. Understand that?"

"Yes, ma'am," I said. I loved hearing that message.

Sure enough, a few days later another incident occurred. Some kid called me dirty names. I doubled up my fist, but before I could hit him, he started to run home. I chased him to his apartment building. He pushed open the hallway door, and I was right behind him. I grabbed him just as he opened his own door and hit him as hard as I could.

"Daddy! Daddy! Help!" he screamed and called me more dirty names.

I hit him again.

The boy's dad rushed into the front room, saw me, and pushed open the door. He pulled his son inside, and then he picked me up. He seemed like a really big man, but I was so small I have no idea how large he really was. He carried me down the hallway and out the back door of the building. He shoved me outside.

"Hey! Leave him alone!" screamed Fred, who only saw the man pushing me out the door. The man ignored Fred and went back inside his apartment.

Fred came up to me and put his arm on my shoulder. "What happened?" he asked.

After I told him, his first words were "Let's tell Mama." Together we raced home.

Mom was in her ninth month of pregnancy with her eighth child. She wasn't feeling well, and she didn't need us rushing inside and upsetting her. But feeling ill didn't stop Mama from defending her boys. Less than a minute later, she marched out of our apartment, carrying a baseball bat in her left hand. "Which apartment?" was all she asked.

I took her there and stood to the side when she knocked on the door with the bat. The startled man opened the door to see a bat waving in his face.

"You picked up my son and threw him outside. Shame on you."

"I didn't touch him."

"Yes, you did! You could have hurt him bad. You're a man, and he's only a small boy. Besides, you had no idea what your boy did first." She went on and on, and the man just stared at her.

"I didn't do anything," the man said again, but not very confidently.

Mama glared at him. She knew he was lying, but she said, "You won't ever touch one of my kids again. Is that clear?"

He nodded that time.

"All right boys, let's go home." Mom took us back to our apartment and told us to sit down.

The lines in her face told me how much strength the incident had taken from her. I felt bad about that. "I want you to learn something from this," she said slowly. "You see, he did a bad thing. Then he made it worse because he lied. He picked you up, and he knew I knew it. I could see it in his eyes, but he wasn't man enough to admit he had done wrong. Let that be another lesson, boys. I always want you to admit it when you've done something wrong. Don't lie to me. Lying only makes things worse."

Afterward, I thought about what Mama had said. I hadn't lied to her about some of the fights; I just hadn't told her everything. As I thought about those provoked fights, I admitted to myself that I had done wrong. I promised God and I promised myself that I wouldn't do anything like that again.

My mother lost the baby. I don't think the confrontation with the nasty father had anything to do with it. The baby had a prolapsed cord. Mom's water broke at home. Because she had already had seven children, she knew it wasn't time to go to the hospital. This time was different, because when her water broke, the cord came out. The baby was breech, feet fist. When Mom's water broke, the baby's feet pushed the umbilical cord out. By the time she went into labor, the baby—a boy they named Joseph—had died. If he had been her first child, she might have insisted on going to the hospital earlier, which might have saved him.

Later that same night, while Mom stayed in the hospital, Dad came home and called us together. "Get all the stuff together that your mother made or bought for the baby," he said. He told us to put it in boxes and hide everything in the front closet. "It will just make her sadder to see all those things that were to be part of a happy homecoming with a new baby."

When Mom came home, she was sad. So was Dad. We were too young to understand how devastating such a loss was. We knew only that our parents hardly smiled for what seemed like a long time. We had lived in a happy, fun-filled house, and suddenly the volume went down. Hardly anyone talked. Maybe we just didn't know what to say. We didn't whisper, but we did everything very quietly for several days.

Years later, Dad still talked about Joseph's death. One time before he died, Dad said, "We were expecting a baby, and nobody showed up." Tears filled his eyes. All those years and the loss still hurt.

Joseph's death was the saddest moment of our childhood. It was also a time when we reached out to each other for comfort. I don't think we realized what we were doing, but we were standing together in our common grief. This was part of our bonding that remains even today.

This habit started at home.

Chapter 5

Sharing and Caring Creates a Better You

Each child is responsible for the next younger child.

I was too young to remember the birth of Deborah, the third child in our family, but I clearly remember when the twins were born on February 6, 1955. Like most twins, they arrived prematurely and underweight. Babies had to weigh five pounds before they could go home, so Michael stayed in the hospital ten days and Mitchell remained there an additional four.

When Michael came home, Fred held out his arms for the baby. "Let me have him. He's mine. I'm going to take care of him." Fred, who was calm and quiet even then, spoke in such a way that his words settled the matter. He had claimed Michael as his responsibility.

"That's good, son," Dad said and patted his shoulder.

Not to be outdone, when Mitchell came home I claimed him. "I'll take care of him. I promise," I told my parents.

"That's a good thing to do," Dad said and smiled at me.

Fred was six and I was five, but we felt like parents ourselves. Somehow Mom and Dad had already taught us the importance of being responsible for those younger than we were. I don't recall that we ever resented taking care of the twins. If anything, we wanted to do more for them.

I'm not sure Fred and I did all that much, but we felt as if we were making big contributions. We changed the babies' diapers. We held them when they cried. We took care of things like heating the baby formula for Mom.

Even though we tried to take care of the twins as much as possible, Fred and I never felt neglected. Our parents found ways to let us know they appreciated what we were doing. Sometimes Mom gave me a smile, a quick hug, or just a simple "Thank you for doing that."

When Dad said, "You boys are doing a good job in helping out," those words made us want to do even more.

As I've already mentioned, each week we had to memorize a Bible verse for Sabbath school. The older children helped the younger ones with their lessons. Every morning before we left for school, we read part of the church lesson and went over it again at night. As soon as he was able to read well, Fred helped me. When I reached third grade, I helped Deborah, and when she was able to read, she worked with the twins. Of course, sometimes a section was so difficult that one of the twins appealed to Fred or to me.

The matter of the lessons also illustrates the principle we learned to live by from our earliest days. Each child's being responsible for the younger worked all the way down to Freda's being responsible for Ruthie, who was three years younger.

As part of this plan, the oldest child was in charge if our parents weren't available. For instance, everybody younger than Fred had to listen to him. When I was the oldest one at home, all the others had to listen to me.

That's not all. Our parents also built in a system of accountability. If the older ones didn't treat the younger ones right, the little kids complained to our parents. That meant we older kids received rebukes for our wrongdoing. Fred was so easygoing and yet, like Dad, he got what he wanted by staying calm and saying what he wanted. I tended to be dictatorial. When my turn came, I demanded and expected them to do what I said. That brought resentment. The others told me, "We don't like it when you're in charge."

This system made sense even though I had not heard of it in other families. "Your daddy and I could get killed in a car accident," Mom said. "If you behave and look out for one another, nobody will mind helping you."

We not only learned that system, but we still live by it. Until Fred's death in a plane crash in 1994, whenever any problems came up that affected the whole family, all of us went to him first. Since the accident they come to me as the oldest. It's a matter of trusting each other and going to whoever is next oldest.

This is especially true when two siblings disagree. Suppose Ruth and Freda have a difference of opinion. They're the two youngest, so they go to Dyfierd. That older child settles the dispute, and that's the end of it. If the older can't settle the difference, the younger goes up the age chain until one of us can end the conflict. I don't remember that anyone has ever had to go up the entire chain, but that's the principle we worked on.

Mitchell remembers a day when, during his teen years, he was sick and stayed in bed. Our mother had gone out on an errand. Dad had to leave for the base. That meant that Mitch would be without either of our parents for only a short time, perhaps half an hour. The younger siblings were there, and he, being the oldest one home, was in charge of the others even though he was sick.

Heavy rain had fallen all day, and weather reporters kept calling for a tornado watch in the area—something that had never happened in Fayetteville, North Carolina.

Just then, Mitchell heard a terrific wind blowing. He described it as the sound of a train—and it was growing louder. As sick as he was, he jumped out of bed, raced over to the door, and opened it. As he stared at the blackening sky, he spotted a funnel cloud heading right toward our home.

"Hit the floor!" he screamed like a military commander. "Take cover immediately." He dove for the floor, and the younger kids followed his lead.

The tornado sprayed glass across the front of the house. Winds ripped a tree up by the roots in our front yard and took off part of our roof. In our neighborhood, the storm lifted cars and moved them hundreds of yards. Other houses had minor damage, mostly shattered glass.

"I'm convinced that because Mom and Dad had taught all the kids to obey the older one in charge, my brothers and sisters were saved," Mitchell says. "I really appreciate that lesson. In fact, we still look after each other today, and we will call one another to get the opinion of the other when making decisions in life. As a result, we've all been helped in our jobs."

Even today, Mitchell might call Dyfierd and ask his advice. Freda might call me. That's how we are. Because we learned to watch out for each other, we depend on one another and value each other's knowledge and skills. That has helped all of us in working through many problems and has allowed us to be successful.

As in any family, squabbles erupted over small things such as toys or who could sit in which chair. Our parents insisted that we share everything. Other than clothes, we had no sense of private property. Everything belonged to the family.

We had a rule about toys that I learned when I was about eight. It didn't matter what I had; if I was playing with something and a younger child wanted it, I was to surrender the toy.

I learned that lesson the hard way. One day when Mabel was less than two years old, we were playing outside. I had a rubber ball and was bouncing it against the tree and then running to catch it.

"Give me the ball," Mabel said.

"When I'm finished."

"Give me the ball."

Dad was standing by, and he said, "Larry, give her the ball."

I knew the rule, of course, but I didn't always think it was fair and said so. "I had it first, and she only wants the ball because I have it," I protested.

"That's true," Dad said, "but you're older, and you should be able to understand. Mabel is younger, and she hasn't learned the importance of sharing. She'll figure it out one day. Do you know why she'll finally understand sharing?"

"No, sir."

"Because you're teaching her. Just like right now. You share with her and she'll learn to share with others."

He was right again, of course. Another Harris principle took root: family, not individual wants, was first.

Chapter 6

Family Members Are Friends for Life

Your best friends are your family members.

All through my growing-up years, Mom stressed that the family is the most important thing and that our best friends should be our siblings. "You need to be close to one another, because Mom and Dad may not always be around. Then you'll need each other's support."

Here's another way Mom emphasized the importance of family relationships: "You may have a friend for fifteen years, then some problem happens, and the friendship is over. In the family, even if you have disagreements and differences, it won't matter. The family is always there, and that's all you really have."

We did become each other's best friends and still are, even as we are now reaching middle age. We see and talk to each other by phone frequently, sometimes daily.

Because we were friends even as children, family vacations were especially fun. Today I can't figure out how we did it, but all eleven of us traveled in one car. What a challenge it was to our parents to find places to stack our suitcases along with all of us. Somehow they got everything inside or on top.

To us, those family vacations meant adventure. We got away from Fayetteville for a week or more. We were together, and we traveled with our best friends. What better vacation could we have had?

When Michael and Mitchell were accepted at Duke University in Durham, North Carolina, I was as excited as they were. I was a graduate student in the university's medical school, so all three of us roomed together. We loved sharing the same apartment. In fact, just being together was a little like living at home. None of us felt lonely, because we had two others with us.

The twins and I stayed together in a campus apartment the second, third, and part of the fourth year. We had a wonderful time. We divided the labor, and Michael and Mitch did most of the cooking. Neither of them could ever become a chef. In fact, most of the time their cooking was barely edible, despite all the training they had received at home.

It wasn't uncommon for us to splurge at Dunkin' Donuts at one o'clock in the morning, then hurry back to the apartment to study some more. We lived together happily because we were, above all things, friends.

I developed my life philosophy through my strong family ties and friendship with my siblings: "Nothing comes easy. Life is about ups and downs, successes and failures. How well we survive depends on how well we can get up when we fall down. The love of God and the love of family are the hydraulic jacks that we need to lift us up."

Deborah says it this way: "As a team, our parents showed us the value of working together, helping one another, and encouraging one another. They expected nothing but the best. They supported us but never condoned our wrongs. Our parents shared their responsibilities and respected each other's role and contribution." She adds, "We're all still best friends."

We all went to the colleges of our choice. Our parents didn't have the money to pay our way, although they helped as much as they could. We had all studied diligently in school. That hard work paid off in scholarships, loans, and work-study jobs.

In fact, I didn't worry about money while I was in college. I never had any, but I didn't feel deprived. That's one of the joys of coming from the Harris family—we didn't need to have things to feel content and secure. We had each other. Perhaps that sounds like a cliché, but it was true. Each of us had the sense that we could turn to a sibling or to our parents and somehow everything would be all right. Our faith in God, of course, was a large part of that.

All nine of us started out as best friends, and we've continued that way. Perhaps that's not fully clear, so I want to share a few experiences in which we've demonstrated this continued closeness.

First, in the 1980s after Fred had finished his military obligation, he opened his own dental practice. The economy wasn't good, and he soon found himself almost at the point of bankruptcy. Fred made several mistakes. He had been in the army and didn't understand all the intricacies of going into private practice. For instance, he made partials or full dentures for patients. Instead of asking for payment in advance, Fred had them made and then sometimes the patients wouldn't or couldn't pay. Then he lost money because he couldn't return the dentures. He hadn't figured on the high prices for lab work, and he had underestimated the cost of dental equipment. We didn't care about his mistakes; we cared about Fred. I could only think of him as my older brother and my best friend. He needed me, and I wouldn't let him down, regardless of the reasons for his problems.

After Fred's business hit bottom, we had an opportunity to rush to his aid. At that time, my wife, Bertie, and I were the most able to help financially. Without ever questioning the wisdom of our actions, we did what we could, because my best friend was about to lose everything.

We put up our office building as collateral. I was already established as a pediatrician, so I was able—and delighted—to help my big brother. For a period of about two years, until Fred was able to get his finances straightened out, Bertie and I made his loan payments. They were $2,500 a month, and that was a lot of money. This may sound strange, but Bertie and I never talked about the amount. Our concern was doing enough for Fred. I loved my brother and would have done anything for him. We would have carried him longer if he had needed the help.

One of my colleagues learned what I had done, and he referred to the "sacrifice" I had made.

"This was no sacrifice," I responded. "This was a privilege. Wouldn't you do this for your best friend? Even if I hadn't loved him that much, I would have done it. We are family. We stand up for each other—an early life lesson in the Harris family."

"I wish I had a brother like that," he said.

I didn't say it, but I thought, *I have eight brothers and sisters like that. They'd rush to my aid just as quickly as I rushed to Fred's.* Many times I remembered how Fred had protected me from boys who wanted to beat me in fights. When they were picking on me, he didn't care who started the fight.

The friendship of family continues with 6 spouses and 15 grandchildren: The Harris brood after a reunion breakfast, Fayetteville, NC, July 4, 1987.

He cared only about helping me. In a way, loaning Fred the money was like repaying a favor.

A second instance: In 1998 Dyfierd, who is a career army officer, was promoted to colonel and became the battalion commander at Fort Hood, Texas. All of us wanted to go to his inauguration ceremony. I was the only sibling not able to attend, and I grieved over that. I felt as if I were letting my brother down (although I knew Dyfierd didn't feel that way), and I knew I was missing something very special in his life. I couldn't go because at that time I had a solo practice and I couldn't find anyone to take my place.

Third, in May 1999, Dyfierd's twin daughters, Adrienne and Angelique, graduated from high school. Just before their graduation, however, the army sent Dyfierd to Bosnia.

That was shortly after the breakup of Yugoslavia, and there was a lot of tension and danger in the area.

That transfer meant he couldn't attend his daughters' graduation. Dyfierd called that event one of the greatest disappointments of his life. "I cried like a baby," he said. He describes it this way:

> I have missed many events in my children's lives, but I never imagined I would miss the high school graduation of my twin daughters. It was one of the most difficult things I have had to do in my life. I still remember that morning when I woke up in Bosnia. It was a quiet day, and there weren't many of those. My thoughts switched to home, and I thought about my family. My emotions overcame me, and I yearned to go home and be with them. Yet I knew I couldn't.
>
> I commanded a battalion task force with more than 330 people, and an air war was going on near us. I thought about my father and wondered how many times he must have felt that deep loneliness that every soldier knows when he has to be separated from loved ones. What about my children, my baby girls, and my wife? Would they understand why I couldn't be with them?
>
> I knew they would, but that didn't lessen the sadness. I had to drive on. I was in Bosnia because it was my profession, my calling, and my sacrifice. I credit my parents' examples of sacrifice and commitment for helping me to "soldier up" so I could stay focused and lead my battalion.

Although the twins' father couldn't be with the girls, some of us could. Mom hates to fly, but she went to the graduation anyway. Not all of us could get away, but most of us were there, because this was a special occasion. Our best friend's daughters graduated, and we wanted to stand in his place.

Fourth, when we were in high school, Fred and I cut lawns every summer. We worked together without any problems and split the money evenly. When Fred turned fifteen he was able to take driver's education classes that summer. This meant that for two weeks, he left for school in the mornings, and I went out alone to cut the grass.

After his absence, I handed Fred his half of the money for cutting grass.

"I can't take that, it's yours. You did all the work," he said.

I shook my head. "We're a team. If I got to go to driver's ed, wouldn't you share with me what you earned without my help?"

"Of course I would."

I laughed because I had made my point.

Neither of us thought about saying, "I did more work than you did." In fact, if one of my friends hadn't made a point of it, telling me how foolish it was for me to work while Fred was in school, I wouldn't even have thought of it.

"But he's my brother," I said, "and besides, he's my best friend." That ended the discussion.

Finally, Michael had suffered from diabetes for a long time and had been on dialysis for several years. He was getting worse. It became obvious to me that only a kidney transplant would save his life. I think Michael knew it too, but he was proud and stubborn—just like Dad had been when he refused help with Christmas gifts when we lived in Germany. Michael felt that he could take care of himself without being a burden to his siblings. "I have to keep driving on," he said once.

In 2000 he reached the crisis point. Dialysis was no longer working efficiently, and he was near death. That's when Mom finally had a long talk with him. She helped him realize that he wasn't making it hard on us. In fact, he was making it hard on himself.

"Mom's right," he said. "We are a family and we stick together, no matter what—just like we've always done." He finally said that he would accept a kidney transplant.

The most obvious solution was for one of his siblings to donate a kidney. All of us wanted to be the one, but not all of us could. I had diabetes, so the doctors wouldn't consider me as a candidate. His twin also had diabetes, so that eliminated him. Mabel was compatible, but she had high blood pressure, so they rejected her.

Of Michael's seven surviving siblings, the only one compatible to donate was Dyfierd. Although he had no health problems, he was a career military officer—a colonel. The removal of a kidney could have left him debilitated. Dyfierd flies an Apache attack helicopter, and his work puts him at risk for back and kidney injuries. He squarely faced the reality that he would have only one kidney. If he were injured in a crash, for instance, he would have no backup.

To make Dyfierd's situation more tense, he had his own family to think about. At the time his three children were all in college, which involved a lot of expense. If something happened to him, it would affect their careers.

Dyfierd considered the hazards to his own health but put those thoughts behind him. He knew the surgery could put his military career in jeopardy, but giving a kidney to his best friend came first.

In October of 2000, all of us siblings flew or drove to Atlanta's Piedmont Hospital for Michael's surgery. The transplant was a success.

Dyfierd puts the experience in these words:

> The sacrifice I am most proud of is the one I shared with my brother Michael. On 31 October 2000, we both underwent kidney surgery; I was the donor.
>
> Before I could donate my kidney, I underwent tests at Fort Rucker, Alabama. A young soldier asked, "Why are you donating your kidney to your brother?"
>
> I stared at him uncomprehendingly. "Michael is my brother, that's why," I said.
>
> "I wouldn't do that for my brother."
>
> I could hardly believe what I heard. How could this soldier be willing to sacrifice for total strangers, I wondered, yet not be willing to do the same for his own flesh and blood?
>
> If I had thought about it a little longer, I think I would have said, "I'm doing what I know is right. My family comes first, and this is one of the proudest moments of my life. This is a gift of love to my brother. I can give him the gift of life."

To me, as the oldest living brother, the best thing about Michael's transplant was the total support of the family for him. He knew that all of us had wanted to give and that each of us would have if it had been possible. That experience reminded me of how deeply all of us love each other. After all, we're best friends.

Chapter 7

You Learn
How to Give
from Family

Always be willing to give to those less fortunate.

Today my four sisters work with children. Fred became a dentist, and I became a pediatrician. The twins tried to get into medical school, but they did not get accepted, so they chose to work for pharmaceutical companies. In our own way, each of us reaches out to help others as our way to alleviate suffering. As Mom says, "You're still holding on to the Lord, working actively in the church, and you're showing it by helping those in need."

Although we were a family of eleven and committed to each other, our upbringing taught us to do whatever we could for other people. "Always be willing to give to those who are less fortunate than you are," both parents said.

We never had much money, but none of us missed any meals or felt deprived. We didn't consider ourselves poor, because we felt so secure, surrounded by loving parents and siblings who would do anything they could for each other.

Our parents ingrained in us that helping others was our privilege and responsibility. They didn't judge other families' decisions or money management. Sometimes, however, they pointed out to us that we needed to be careful not to make the same mistakes.

We in the Harris family had little money, but we learned to take care of ourselves and to remember that there were always others worse off. While we were quite young, we learned we could help others through acts of kindness. Giving money was only one method.

I think that our cleaning up the church after any activity was part of that. I don't remember Mom and Dad ever talking about the reason for doing it. We just organized ourselves and went to work. During our growing-up years, Dad didn't belong to the church, but that didn't stop him from helping whenever he could. Many people came to church suppers, ate, and left immediately. That was all right, because we honestly didn't mind staying there to clear and wipe tables, sweep up, and empty the garbage until everything was clean.

Doing that was like doing our chores at home. We cleaned up because it was the right thing to do. Even today, we're not often in charge of the activities at church, but we still stick around and clean up. We wouldn't feel right not doing that.

We also learned that when we help others, sometimes people will take advantage of us. One thing my parents taught us, however, is that when we do kind things for others, we are really doing them for Jesus Christ.

Just to give an example of my parents' attitude toward sharing with others, I remember when my dad bought his first new car, a 1965 Nash Rambler. He was truly proud of that new car and, of course, so were we.

The same day Dad brought the Nash home, one of my uncles came over to our house and asked to borrow it. He needed to drive to Washington, D.C.

Without the slightest hesitation, Dad handed him the car keys.

Our uncle left his car with us—an older Rambler. He also gave very specific instructions on who could sit in which seat.

"Dad, how could you do that?" I was a bigmouthed teenager and shocked by the whole thing. (I was also a little angry that my uncle had been so fussy about who could sit where.) "You loaned him your brand-new car!"

The other children who were home also raised objections, but Dad only smiled. "Well, you never know. If you treat people right, one day that goodness might come back to you."

That was probably the most startling example I can remember from childhood. Dad had worked hard to earn the money to make the down payment on that Nash Rambler. I hated the fact that Dad hadn't put even one hundred miles on the car yet, but that thought probably never occurred to him.

We never had a lot, as I've made clear, but that never stopped our sharing. Occasionally, new, young soldiers came into Fayetteville and attended our church. After worship services, they didn't have homes to go to, so their only choice was to head back to the base. Many times Mom invited them to share our dinner, and we always had enough. When we were in college, Mom did the same thing for students whenever she saw any of them in need.

Our parents' example rubbed off on me and on all of us. It's just a principle we all live by: We help others.

Mitchell says:

> This isn't to brag, but giving is just part of our way of life. The Bible teaches the giving of 10 percent—the tithe—but our parents taught us to double that out of gratefulness to God.
>
> As a family and as individuals, we help pay tuition for kids who don't have scholarships so they can get into college. When we've heard of people without electricity or a car

that won't run, we do what we can. Sometimes we've loaned money, and even as we did it, we didn't expect repayment. We did it because our parents taught us kindness.

First John 3:17 states that if we see a brother or sister experiencing hardship and don't do what we can, we don't have Jesus' love in us. I don't want to be guilty of turning my back on genuine need. I also don't want to be taken advantage of; but if I have to err on one side, I'd rather be taken advantage of than turn away a truly needy person.

This is an issue that involves more than money. One day, for instance, we closed the clinic at the regular hour. Maybe thirty minutes later I heard a banging at the back door. When I opened it, a mother stood there with her child. "She's sick. Please help her."

I could have said, "Take her to the emergency ward," but that didn't occur to me. I could see the baby was quite ill.

I said, "Come on in." I was only following the example I had learned at home.

I remember how we recycled clothes in our family. Sometimes we had clothes that were still good but no one wanted to wear them. This was especially true with my sisters. Mom often took those clothes to her sister, who had eleven children and didn't seem to do as well as we did. I know that many times Mom took them food or other things. She didn't tell us, but we saw her doing it.

Maybe that's as important as anything. Our parents did kind, generous things for others, and we observed their deeds. Seeing their caring in action probably taught me more about being kind to others than anything else.

We don't restrict our giving just to needs around us. Every year Michael donates money to an organization that provides mopeds for ministers in Africa because they have to walk twenty or thirty miles between churches.

We're all active in our church's programs. We're there to assist kids in any way we can. For instance, we like to help local schools and boys' and girls' organizations. I regularly help buy uniforms for a church basketball team and equipment and uniforms for city sports programs for the underprivileged. My siblings and I endow a scholarship at a local high school in memory of my brother Fred.

I suppose it all comes down to this: We never forget where we came from. Mom said we could grow up to be whatever we wanted to be, but we mustn't forget our roots. "Always go back," she says. "Reach out to help each other."

I don't mean that we're stupid and give to just anyone. Our parents taught us to make decisions. There are people who come around every year and want something. They don't seem to do anything to help themselves. That's not what I mean. We try to see genuine needs and help.

Here are two examples.

First, almost every year I sponsor a children's tennis tournament. When the word gets around about my sponsorship, adults come to ask me to sponsor tournaments for them. I refuse. "I'm not sponsoring anything for adults. I'm doing it for kids, because they can't do it themselves."

Second, when I first started my practice, I worried about some of the parents. I prescribed medication and then worried that they couldn't afford to buy what the child needed. Sometimes I wrote the prescription and sent them to a nearby drugstore where I had an account. The pharmacist charged it to me.

One day, however, a young mother came in with her baby and said, "I need some Tylenol. Do you have any?"

I had learned that every time that woman came in, she would ask me for something. She never did anything to provide for herself or her baby. Therefore, I didn't feel that giving more would help her.

"No, I don't have any Tylenol to give away," I said. "Why don't you go out and buy some?"

"I don't have any money."

"What about your baby's daddy?"

"I don't know where he is."

"What about the grandparents?"

"They ain't got no money neither. What am I supposed to do?"

I had heard this kind of talk from that mother so many times that I really lost control that day. She was on welfare and made no attempt to find a job. I asked, "Did you give birth to this baby?"

"Sure I did."

"You're her mother. Go out and do some work so you can buy Tylenol. Once you make a decision to do something like have a child, then you've got to be willing to sacrifice."

"Sacrifice? I don't have anything to sacri—"

"You're wearing lipstick. You smoke cigarettes, because I can smell the odor on you. You probably eat at McDonald's. Save some of that money and buy Tylenol."

"Well, my friend went to another doctor," she said, "and he gave her Tylenol. Didn't cost her nothing."

"If we had samples, I'd give them to you. But I'm not going to go buy Tylenol for you. That's your responsibility."

She stared at me uncomprehendingly, then left very angry.

At first I felt bad, and then I remembered that my dad used to say there are always people who want everything free. "If you want something," I heard him say many times, "then you have to work for it."

People have occasionally taken advantage of me. For instance, one time a man came to my office. "I remember you, Dr. Harris, because you took care of my kids and you were always good to us." Then he said, "I don't have any money, and my car needs towing to a garage."

I must have mumbled something about being sorry.

"You see, Dr. Harris, I don't get paid until tomorrow, and I have to have my car repaired. If you'll loan me twenty-five dollars, I'll repay you—I promise—when I get paid tomorrow."

I believed him and gave him the money.

Minutes later he came back. "They told me that the fee has gone up to forty dollars." I handed him another fifteen dollars. "Don't you worry. I'll be back at this time tomorrow and pay every cent."

I never saw that man again. Even though he lied to me and cheated me, I do believe his need was real, and my parents taught me to help those in need. I still think I did the right thing.

Occasionally, I'll meet men I grew up with, and they'll say, "I'm hungry, Larry. Will you give me two dollars for a sandwich?"

"I'll do better than that," I say. I go inside the store and buy a sandwich. Before I leave the store, I say to the clerk, "Don't let him bring it back and get the money for it." I don't want anyone to go hungry, but I don't want to pay for anyone's liquor habit either.

As I've already mentioned, my mother worked for Treasure City for years, but she didn't really find her place in the workforce until she became a teacher's assistant. That's where she felt she could help children. By then, she had her high school diploma. Dad had gotten his GED and gone on to graduate from college after all of us were out of the home; Mom just didn't have those opportunities. But she did know how to give. Helping in the classroom was one major way for her to do so.

This is one experience I want to share in Mom's own words:

> One day in the classroom I saw a second-grade boy who was getting ready to pull the chair from under a little girl as she sat down.
>
> "You don't do that," I said and pulled him away. "She could fall and break her neck."
>
> "Well, I was going to sit there, and I was only trying to take the chair for myself."
>
> "I don't care. First, she's a girl, and you need to be courteous to her. Second, she could have gotten hurt."
>
> "Oh, who you talking to?" Before I had a chance to reply, he noticed the dark circles under my eyes. "I'll knock all that black from under your eyes."
>
> "Yes, and they will bury you with your head still in the air, Son. I've raised five boys and four girls. Nobody ever hit me, and it's not going to start with you."
>
> "Oh, I get your drift." He sat right on down.
>
> I never had any more trouble from him the rest of the year.

Here's another story she told me.

> The child I most remember was a little boy that the system had labeled as EMH—educationally mentally handicapped. The

assistant principal brought him into the classroom and said to the teacher, in the boy's presence, "This kid is bad. He's not going to amount to anything. He's not going to learn, so just do whatever you can with him until the school year's over."

I felt really sad that anyone thought that way and even sadder that she said it in front of the boy. I also thought, *Nobody is so bad that he can't be reached.* I didn't say anything then.

Later that day, the teacher asked me to help that boy with his reading. I sat down on the floor beside him. "What's your problem with reading? I want to help."

"I don't have to read. I can do whatever I want to do in here."

"Is that what you did last year?"

He nodded.

"Well, that's not going to happen this year."

"My mama said you don't teach us nothing anyways, so what does it matter?"

"Your mama is exactly right," I said. "I can't teach you a thing until I teach you what she should have taught you when you were at home: Sit down and be still. If you don't learn anything else this year, you're going to learn to sit down and be still. Do you understand that?"

His eyes widened. I'm sure no one had ever talked to him that way before.

"Yeah." Then he scrunched up his face and yelled, "I hate you!"

"That's all right. I'm not here for a popularity contest. But as long as I'm in here, you will do what I say. Do you understand that?"

He dropped his head and didn't say anything more.

For the rest of the day, I made him sit right beside me while I worked with other children. Every few minutes he started to get up. "Sit down," I said, and then I ignored him.

101

When this boy first came into the classroom, he didn't know anything. He couldn't read. He didn't understand the concept of adding one and one. He'd been playing for two years. But after that day, I didn't have any more trouble with the boy. In fact, he was ready to learn, and he learned fast. By the end of that year he could read on an average level for his age. He could even add two-digit numbers.

On the last day of school he said, "I can even write my own name." Then he started telling me other things he could do.

I smiled and laughed with him.

"Know what else I learned? I learned to sit down and be still."

"That's what I told you."

"You know something else, Mrs. Harris? I love you." He gave me a big hug before he left.

It's the trickle-down effect: We saw our parents actively give, so we have patterned a lifestyle of giving based on their example. It all started at home.

Chapter 8

Discipline at Home Does Its Work

Respect each other and respect those older.

Mom smiles when she talks about the early days of child rearing. I don't remember this, but Mom says that when we were barely toddlers, she taught us to pick up things and help each other. If she changed my diaper, she asked Fred to put it in the dirty clothes hamper. She did the same thing with me when Deborah came along. And we all had to put things where they belonged.

A visitor criticized my mother for doing that. "You ought to be ashamed of yourself. You're trying to make slaves out of your children."

"If I let them throw clothes on the floor, then that's where they think they're supposed to go. I'll be picking up clothes all day long. They have to learn." Her friend's remarks may have hurt Mom's feelings, but they didn't change her way of molding our behavior.

Here's another example of the type of discipline exercised in our home. When I was about ten years old, Deborah and I became involved in a scuffle. She threw the first punch, and I hit her back. We had a couple of mild physical exchanges. I was bigger and older, so she was getting the worst of it. She raced from the room and yelled for Dad.

"Larry hit me! Larry hit me!"

I ran right behind her and said, "She started it. She hit me first."

"Let's get one thing straight, Larry. Boys don't hit girls— ever." He explained that once when he was a boy, he hit his sister in the breast and hurt her. After Dad spanked me, he explained, "Son, girls are smaller and physically weaker. They can't hurt you the way a boy can."

As he talked, I remembered that Deborah had hit me pretty hard and it had hurt a lot. But I didn't argue with my father.

"Have you ever seen me hit your mother? Have you ever seen me hit any woman? You do not hit girls. Not ever."

"Yes, sir," I said. Since then I have never hit my sister or any other female.

The end of that story, however, is that later I told Mom what happened. When Deborah admitted she had hit me first, Mom spanked her. I felt justified.

We learned one lesson very early: Respect every adult even if the adult was disrespectful to you. We were told, "You do not talk back to an adult. If an adult does something wrong to you, then you tell us and we'll take care of it."

"You have to take care of yourself, be respectful, and behave yourself," Dad said. "You can't make other people behave, but you don't have to follow their example."

A couple of times I yelled at coaches in games (and usually got expelled from the game), but I always remembered that teaching, and so did my brothers and sisters.

Generally, we didn't talk back to our parents. That attitude didn't grow out of fear or worry that we'd be punished. I don't think sassing occurred to us. At least, not often . . .

When we were young, Fred and I shared a bedroom, and we alternated days on policing it. He was eleven then and decided he didn't want to clean up on his day.

When Dad looked into our room and saw that things hadn't been straightened up and the floor hadn't been swept, he said, "It's your day, Fred. Now get busy and clean up the room."

"I don't want to clean up this old room. I'm tired, and besides, the room looks fine to me."

Dad didn't say anything for what seemed like minutes. Then he slowly shook his head. "Is that nice?" The sad expression on his face spoke louder than anything he said. "I've taken care of you and always treated you right. Think about what you just said. Do you think that's nice?"

Fred hung his head in shame.

"What if I treated you disrespectfully? What if I didn't allow you to do anything you wanted or talked to you that way? You wouldn't like that, would you?"

"No, sir," Fred said.

Dad closed the door. As soon as he was gone, Fred hurriedly cleaned the room. The issue never came up again.

That's the only time in the years we children lived with our parents that I ever heard disrespectful words toward them. By comparison with other families, Fred's momentary rebellion sounds mild, and of course it was. Because Dad handled it lovingly and wisely, Fred knew (and so did I) that he had hurt Dad's feelings. We loved our parents too much to hurt them.

As I've reflected on the strict discipline in our home and how little trouble our parents had enforcing it, I think I know why. They loved us.

Even more important to us, we *knew* we were loved. We didn't talk or even think much about it, but deep inside all of us knew we received their affection. Many times they told us they were teaching us the best way they knew how and that was the way God structured the family.

107

Sometimes we'd see how differently other people raised their kids, such as letting them stay out as late as they wanted. Now and then, we wished we had that kind of freedom, but we didn't feel that way often. Mostly we liked the way our parents treated us. They were fair. Even if we didn't always like what they said, we knew they were usually right.

My mother did most of the spanking, but Dad talked to us, and that was worse. Sometimes he said, "Explain to me the reason you said those words." Or he might say, "Give me two good reasons why I shouldn't spank you."

To know that we had disappointed him hurt much worse than any spanking. We stared at him, but Dad didn't let us move until we gave him two reasons.

Then he said, "How many licks do you think you deserve for that?" Even though he asked, Dad didn't always give the same number we thought we deserved.

Before any of us received our punishment, we were allowed to ask questions. "But no back talk," Mom said.

Both our parents wanted to make certain we understood why we were being punished. After our spanking, Mom always hugged us. Somehow in that simple gesture, she made it clear that she wasn't disciplining in anger or out of frustration. She wanted us to face our own mistakes and the consequences of our actions. But the punishment wasn't over until we heard "I love you."

Only once in my life did I ever observe anger in my dad, and that situation involved Michael. I'm pretty frank and outspoken, but Michael is the one with the unruly mouth. Michael was fussing or grumbling and Dad said, "Be quiet."

Michael just kept on, and Dad told him a second time, "Son, be quiet."

That still didn't stop him. This time Dad yelled, "Michael, if you don't shut up, boy, I'm going to get up and knock you down!"

That shocked every one of us. Dad just did not show anger.

Michael shut up.

Mom handled Michael differently. She told him to shut up, and if he didn't, she told him a second time. If he persisted, she slapped him on the face.

Back then, corporal punishment was common. In fact, I don't think people of my parents' generation even questioned spanking. They didn't beat us, and none of us ever had bruises. More than anything else, they injured our pride. I know their form of discipline worked in our family.

We've all heard experts claim that corporal punishment breeds violence. That may be true in some families, but it wasn't true for us. I remember hearing my mother say to people who criticized her method, "I've spanked all my children, and not one's ever been in jail or in trouble with the law."

She never hit us violently and never without cause. I don't think she ever punished us in anger. Mostly, I remember that after Mom spanked me, she would take me in her arms and stroke my cheek. "Now, do you know why I did that?"

Of course I always knew.

Without doubt, the twins received the most spankings and deserved every one of them. Fred and Mabel received the fewest. They were the two who were most like Dad—calm and thoughtful—and they analyzed the situation before responding.

I was the type of child who would willingly do something wrong and then accept the punishment. When Mom spanked me, I didn't cry until I was ready for her to stop. I learned early that if I let her spank me two times and then screamed as if she were killing me, she stopped.

I also learned that if I didn't cry, she spanked longer. I figured out that if I didn't cry, Mom thought she wasn't getting through to me. I was also the stubborn one, and at times the spanking started as a contest of the wills—I defied her to make me cry. That resolve crumbled quickly, because it didn't take more than a few licks for me to give in.

Years later, Mom confessed that she had been just like me when she was little. She didn't cry until she was ready for her mother to stop. Somehow, I learned from the best.

Fred, who seldom got into trouble, never cried when spanked, almost as if he knew he deserved everything he got. He wasn't defiant like I was. Mom knew the difference between acceptance and defiance.

The spankings weren't bad. Mom used her soft bedroom slippers or a paddle.

Deborah began crying before my mother even struck her. Mom never did give her many licks because of her screaming.

I'm a lot like my mother—very vocal and outspoken. I say what's on my mind, and sometimes I don't think things through. (Then I have to go back later and apologize for harsh statements I've made.)

Even today at the hospital, when somebody does something wrong I speak up quickly. For instance, if the lab technician was supposed to get certain studies back and she didn't return them when promised, I'd say, "That person isn't doing her job," and I'd say it with some irritation. Later, I may realize there were reasons for my getting the reports back later than expected.

If I get upset, it's nearly always because I think a patient isn't getting the proper care. I'm very meticulous when it comes to my patients, but not everybody's like that. Sometimes if a patient has a certain need, staff members will ignore what they consider minor or inconvenient. That's when I get upset. "You can't do that," I say. "This is a patient. We're here to take care of that person."

Again, however, if I later find out I'm wrong, I go back and apologize. I say, "I'm sorry. This is the way I thought it was."

I learned at home the importance of apologizing for being mistaken. My mother often said to me, "If you make a mistake, be man enough to stand up for it. Apologize—don't just keep the feelings inside."

Again, I want to point out that Mom set the example for apologizing. She's in her seventies, but age hasn't changed her principles. Any time she learns she was wrong, she tries to rectify the situation as soon as possible.

When we lived in Germany, one mother allowed her little boy to curse and yell at neighbors.

One day, in Mom's presence, the boy yelled at the maid, "You're stupid and you're ugly!"

"You shouldn't let him talk that way," Mom said to the mother.

111

"Oh, she's just a maid."

"She's a grown woman. She's a person. A human being."

"Oh, he'll outgrow that."

"No, he won't. And it won't be long before he'll talk to you that way." The neighbor woman didn't like what Mom said and walked away.

Less than a week later, Mom was in the PX at the post. The woman and her son came in. The boy wanted to buy something, and the mother kept saying no.

"You're mean! And you're ugly and you're stupid!" the boy screamed.

She grabbed the boy and spanked him hard.

Mom walked up to her (I told you she is outspoken) and said, "Why are you half-killing him now? You let him do it to the maid, and she is a grown woman. You can't let a child disrespect someone else and think the child will respect you. It doesn't work that way."

Mom took my hand, and we left the PX. I don't know the rest of that story, but I don't remember hearing the boy calling anybody names after that.

It may not sound like a big thing, but we had no restricted places in our house. We could go into any room we wanted and play. There were certain things we didn't do, such as walk on beds, chairs, or tables. Not that I didn't try.

"Larry, chairs are made to sit on," Dad said, "tables made to eat on, and beds made to sleep in."

I had to hear that only once.

Mom's sisters constantly nagged her for being too strict with us. One of them said, "Your children aren't going to come home when they get grown because you're too strict."

"They may not," Mom said, "but they're not going to tear up everything I've got before they leave, either."

Which children came home after they were grown? All of us did.

Along that same line, one of my aunts by marriage visited our house one evening and saw all of us kids studying. Silence filled the house except for the turning of a page or the scraping of a chair.

"This house would make you want to learn," she whispered to my mother. She also noticed that when one of us had a problem, we went to an older brother or sister for help.

"They really study together and help each other, don't they?"

I peeked and saw Mom smiling.

Thanksgiving was a special holiday for us. Each year, Dad packed all of us up, and we went to the base to eat. We sat down at one of the tables. We were aware at an early age that we were the best-behaved kids in the place. In fact, I think it made us feel proud because we didn't cry or scream. For us, it was like eating a meal at home—only we had more choices.

The wife of the base commander stopped and chatted with my parents. "How in the world do you get those children to sit down? Mine would have torn this place up. I'd just rather leave mine at home."

I could see that Mom wanted to tell the woman that the problem was hers and not the children's, but she didn't. She smiled, thanked the woman, and said, "Yes, I have good kids—really good kids."

When we reached the driving age, Mom didn't start laying down all kinds of rules about what we could and couldn't do.

Instead, she said, "The first speeding ticket you get before you're eighteen, that means your license belongs to me. Then you won't have it anymore."

When Mom tells people that, she says, "I meant that about taking their licenses away, and they knew it. But you know, I didn't have any children get a speeding ticket until they were on their own."

One of Mom's most cherished memories of us was when Fred came home from college after his first semester.

"Mama, I thank you for the training you gave me," he said and hugged her. "I look at some of my classmates. Some of them don't attend half the classes, and they go to wild parties. I wonder why they're there."

They talked a few minutes and Fred added, "I guess they didn't have any discipline or training when they were home, so they're just wild now."

Michael told us that a woman came to their church and began speaking about mean mamas. "How many of you had a mama who was mean? All your friends could do something or go someplace, but she wouldn't let you do it or go there?"

As Michael listened, he smiled and thought, *You must have talked to my mama.*

"How many of you had a mama who made you work hard, like wash dishes? When you didn't do something right, she'd throw it all back?"

I know that woman talked to my mama.

The woman talked several minutes and gave many examples of the mean mama, and then she said, "Okay, those of you who had the mean mamas, raise your hands."

Many hands went up.

"How many of you are successful today?"

Almost all those same hands went back up.

"That's the reason you are successful—because you had that mean mama. She taught you good self-discipline, and she taught you how to do things right. That's why you're successful today."

As soon as church was over, Michael called Mom and said, "I just called to thank you for being a mean mama."

In the Harris home, discipline did its work. Respect in our family was a winning way of life.

Chapter 9

The Consequences of Choice Begin in Childhood

Don't compromise to be recognized. You'll be recognized because you don't compromise.

I don't remember hearing the word *integrity* in our house, but that was the focus of most of what our parents taught us. For example, they stressed that we must be truthful. We received stronger punishment for lying than any other bad thing we ever did.

Perhaps because Mom was so honest, we were rarely deceitful. If anything, Mom was a little too honest. I know, because everyone says I'm the most like her. As I've said, like Mom, sometimes in being truthful I haven't always been kind—and then I have to go back and apologize.

One time when we were talking about lying, Fred said, "I don't know how to lie. It shows on my face when I try." I think that's true about all of us.

"It's better to tell the truth and face wrongs than to try to cover them up," Ruth says. "That was a lesson I never forgot."

"Your word is your bond," Dad used to say. "If you tell somebody you're going to do something, you ought to do it. If you promise to pay somebody something, you ought to pay. If you don't pay, then you're lying. If you can't do what you promise, you need to call and talk to them and let them know why."

One time, Freda didn't turn in a homework assignment, and the teacher sent a note home with her. Because she was embarrassed, Freda forged Mom's signature. Later, when my mother went to the PTA, the teacher mentioned how sorry she was that she had had to send home such a note.

"What note was that?" Mom asked.

After the teacher explained, Mom apologized for Freda and said, "She signed the note herself. But don't you punish her. I'll take care of that. She won't do it again—and she won't ever miss handing in another paper, either."

That evening Freda heard a long lecture about lying and being deceitful.

This isn't just a story told from memory. One of my brothers actually tape-recorded the session where Mom confronted Freda.

"I didn't raise any rogues in this family, and that includes liars," Mom said. "None of my kids is going to be a liar."

Then Mom spanked her. Freda howled, although it was obvious she wasn't hurt.

Just then the doorbell rang. One of the twins looked out the window and recognized a deputy sheriff in uniform. "See, Mama, the sheriff is coming to arrest you," he yelled, "because you're spanking Freda!"

"I don't care who comes here," Mom said. "If you lie, you'll steal. I won't have that kind of behavior in this house."

We learned the deputy was attempting to deliver a jury summons and couldn't find the right house. We all laughed, but we learned something through that incident: No one could intimidate our mother when she knew she was right. Her integrity was more important than what people thought about her.

Mom and Dad both stressed that we must behave outside the house the same way we did at home, and we knew how to behave at home. "You may think you're getting away with something," Mom said, "but there'll always be someone out there watching you. You're a Harris, and if you can do it, so can they. People will learn from you."

Mabel says that lesson made a strong impression on her. Today she's a program specialist for child development at Fort Bragg army base. She says that others on the staff trust her. They know she's truthful.

More than once she has heard the comment, "You're different." If staff members tell her something in confidence, she doesn't pass it on. They have seen her integrity in the way she lives and works with them. Because of that, she's been able to counsel and witness to many of her coworkers.

It wasn't just Mom's teaching. Dad believed that if children understood at an early age what their parents expected of them, they would grow up to make the right decisions. "For every choice you make there's a consequence," he often said. When we did make a bad decision, we usually understood the consequences—and vowed not to repeat it.

By the time we had reached our teens, Fred and I wanted to hang out with a group of boys at a shopping mall. Those were kids we went to school with. They invited us to become part of their group, and I guess it was a little flattering.

"Where you boys going?" Mom asked one evening as Fred and I opened the front door and started to leave the house.

"To the mall," Fred said.

"To see some of our friends," I added.

"You boys can go there if you have something to buy, but you don't go there just to hang out." She paused and stared at us.

Both of us lowered our heads. "But Mom—"

"That's how kids get in trouble: nobody supervising them and no one watching over them."

"We won't stay long," I said weakly. I already knew it was a losing battle.

Mom shook her head. "You don't do that! Your name is Harris." We turned around and came back into the house.

For a few minutes, I did feel disappointed. I wondered why we couldn't be like other kids and do the things we wanted. Then I realized that Mom was right. We didn't belong in the mall; in fact, some of our friends had already gotten into minor trouble there.

"Trouble may start small, but it gets bigger if you don't take care of it," Mom once said.

She was right. It just took me a few minutes to admit that fact. I smile sometimes when I remember overhearing Fred say to Deborah, "You have to realize, it's hard to be a Harris."

She laughed and said, "I already know that. They've set high standards for us, haven't they?" Recently Deborah commented about our parents, "They never forced, demanded, or pushed us to hold to those standards, but they loved us and lived by those things themselves. It was only natural that we wanted to please them. Pleasing them meant trying to live by the same standards."

Not everyone understood or approved of the way our family operated. One time a friend of my mother's came over and spent a few hours with her. She saw how we behaved and listened to our discussion about going to a particular activity at school. We chose not to go because it was something we didn't believe in.

"Your children don't participate because they think they're superior to other kids, don't they?" the friend commented.

Shock spread across my mother's face. "Oh, no, that's not true," she said. "They decided not to go. You know why? They've learned not to do things like go to unsupervised parties. I wouldn't stop them if they wanted to go. I've taught them to do what's right, so they're old enough to decide for themselves. It's their choice."

"They act like—"

"No, you see, I want my family to stand for something important. If people don't like it, that's all right as long as the kids are standing for the right things. Not everyone will understand anyway. I've taught my kids that they must not do anything to dishonor their own names or the names of their parents."

I don't know if that woman still thought we felt smug. We know we didn't. We believed we were following our parents and the teachings we learned at church.

As you have seen, we weren't always totally obedient. The twins, for example, were a handful and always into something. Every day they ate breakfast with the rest of us. An hour later, they went next door.

"We're awful hungry," Michael said.

"We'd really like something to eat," Mitchell added.

The neighbor fed them, and that went on for several days. I think she tired of feeding two extra children, so she came to our house and talked to our mother. "Why don't you feed your twins breakfast?"

"I feed those boys every morning. None of my children go hungry."

"Maybe so," the woman said, "but that's not what they've led me to believe. They come over every day and tell me you haven't fed them."

That was the last time the twins went out for breakfast.

Another time, when the twins were perhaps five years old, a neighbor named Mrs. Frances gave them money and sent them to the store to buy bread.

On their way back, Michael, who instigated things, suggested to Mitchell, "Let's fool Mrs. Frances. Let's tell her this is all the change the man gave us." The change was sixty cents—two quarters and a dime. They decided to keep one of the quarters. They handed her thirty-five cents.

When they got home, Michael said, "Let's tell Mama we found this quarter." As soon as they walked inside, Michael held out the coin. "Look, Mama, we found a whole quarter."

"Was there anybody around? Did you see someone drop it?"

"No, Mama," Michael said. "We just found this quarter."

Two days later Mrs. Frances asked my mother, "What did the twins do with my money? I was a quarter short in my change."

"Oh, those rascals have it. They told me they found a quarter. They stole it. But don't you worry, I'll take care of it. They'll bring the money back, and I can promise you that I'll punish them for it, too."

For their lying and stealing, my brothers received one of the sternest lectures and hardest spankings I've ever heard Mom give. Afterwards Mom added, "Anytime you find any money, if somebody is around you ask first."

"Yes, Mama, we promise," Michael said.

About two weeks later, they were visiting in a home and spotted a dime on the floor. They rushed home. "Look, Mama, we found a dime in Mrs. Bivens's house."

"You can't keep that," Mom said. "It's not your money."

"But we didn't see anybody drop it," Michael protested.

"That dime belongs in Mrs. Bivens's house, so that's her money. If you ever find money again, you need to find out whose it is. Otherwise, that's stealing." Once again, she made them take back the money and apologize.

We all learned that lesson clearly. A few years ago, I shopped in a grocery store and when I got home, I discovered items in the grocery bag I knew I hadn't paid for—they were brands I didn't buy. I concluded that the clerk must have put them in my bag by mistake.

When I returned them to the store, the clerk and the manager were both embarrassed. Finally the manager said, "It was our mistake. Just take them."

"No, sir, I can't do that. I didn't pay for them, so they're not mine." I left and let them decide what to do.

Mom used to say, "If you lie, then you will steal. Lying and stealing are just alike." She reminded us, "God is always watching you even when your parents aren't. But people are aware of what you do, and your reputation will follow you forever."

We learned young: Harrises have integrity.

From fairly early, we lived by the principle of choice. We also knew, as our parents reminded us, that we had to consider the consequences of our decisions. All of us seemed to understand why our parents didn't want us to become involved in certain activities. It wasn't because they were sinful, but we learned to ask ourselves, "Where will this lead?"

All through our growing-up years, outsiders tried to tell our parents how to raise us—and some of them couldn't even raise their own children to be respectful. But my parents knew they were teaching us properly. Mom never argued with the would-be counselors but just kept on doing what she knew was the right thing.

I remember once when the style for teens included wide, bell-bottom pants, large-brimmed hats, and stack shoes. In our family, we didn't follow those fads. Again, it was the concept that we never had to compromise by dressing like other kids just to be recognized as part of the crowd. "If you know who you are, it doesn't matter what you wear as long as your clothes are clean."

One neighbor kept harping on us for not dressing like the other kids. "Why don't you let them dress like their friends?" she asked. "You might as well give in now and give them permission. They're going to do it anyway."

"No, we don't have to let them do anything like that," Mom said. "The older kids are working. If they wanted to spend their money on clothes, they could. But I'm not going to encourage them to follow any such fads."

When I heard Mom say that, I lost all desire to dress like other kids. Yes, I had thought about it several times, but I realized that I didn't need to dress a certain way to be accepted. Maybe that's one of the great benefits of being part of our family: We knew our parents loved us and God loved us and we loved each other. We didn't need things to make us feel acceptable.

Mitchell remembers that our parents taught him the decision-making process and that it was important to consider all the facts when making a choice.

> Because I was a twin, Michael often did something wrong and I blindly followed him. When Mom or Dad got ready to punish us, they asked why I did it.
>
> "Because Michael did," was my usual response.

"If your brother jumps in the ocean, are you going to jump in with him?" Mom must have had to say that to me a hundred times.

"No, ma'am."

"We don't do things, especially wrong things, because someone else does them," she said. "Consider the facts and make your own decisions."

That experience paid off in the way the twins behaved. When Michael was in elementary school, one day the teacher left the classroom. Immediately, all the kids started yelling and moving around and making noise. That is, everyone except Michael.

While the teacher was still gone, the principal walked by. He noticed Michael sitting quietly. As a consequence, he told my mom and praised Michael for being such a good boy.

"That's what I mean," Mom said. "We don't have to compromise to be recognized, but we're recognized because we don't compromise." She pointed out to the rest of us that Michael had done the right thing just because it was the right thing.

I've never smoked, and none of my siblings has. We don't drink. None of us ever tried drugs. Those just weren't options for us, and that came out of our religious training. Our parents didn't do any of those things, and they set the right example for us.

I want to make it clear that my parents never forced anything on us. When we were still quite young, they rigidly enforced the principles of honesty, especially telling the truth and not stealing. Once we reached our teens, our parents taught us to make choices. Part of maturing was to reach the place where we chose for ourselves and didn't decide purely based on what Mom or Dad would have done.

For example, of us all, Fred was the most athletic, and he wanted to play football. He was skillful and fast. But his high school played most of their games on our Sabbath. Fred and I talked about whether Mom would allow him to play on that day. He finally asked.

"You're old enough to know what we believe in and whether or not you play on the Sabbath," she said. "It's your decision." She pointed out that she had raised him by godly principles all his life and now it was up to him to make his own choice.

At first, Fred was disappointed that she wouldn't tell him what to do. But it was a powerful spiritual lesson for him. He was the oldest, and in some ways it was the first test of our parents' teaching.

"I'm going to play," he said.

"That's your decision," Mom said, and that was the end of the discussion. She understood what a difficult choice that was for him because Fred loved football and he was good. Coach Carter really wanted Fred on the team. He was sure that he could get Fred a football scholarship.

Fred went out for practice, and the school issued him a uniform. When the time came for him to play his first game on the Sabbath, he was really troubled. He didn't talk to me very much about it, but I knew he had mixed feelings.

"I decided to drop football," he announced. He had made his decision. Like Dad, once he made it, there was no turning back; he just drove on.

Of course, once Fred decided not to play, Mom praised him for making the right decision. She also told us that she had been praying that God would speak to him and help him to make the right choice.

Mabel describes a similar instance:

When I was in college in Greensboro, North Carolina, I decided I wanted to go to one of the nightclubs—one where most of the students hung out on weekends. They filled the place. No one from the family was around, so I knew I could do whatever I wanted. I decided to go there on a Wednesday evening. I went alone and walked into the nightclub. For several minutes, I stood just inside the door and looked around. I listened to the music and some of the conversation and watched the behavior of some of my classmates. I felt out of place. This just isn't me, I thought. It was the only time I had walked into a nightclub, and within minutes I walked right back out.

It wasn't that it was such an evil place. I didn't condemn my classmates for being there. I just knew that, as a Christian, I couldn't be part of that scene.

Two nights later a fight broke out at the same club and several people were hurt. I would have been embarrassed to be seen there or to be part of that group. Yes, for every choice there are consequences.

Mom likes to tell this story about Fred: After he had been in college for almost a semester, she and Dad went to North Carolina A&T State University in Greensboro, North Carolina, to see him. Mom had friends in Greensboro, and she decided to go to the church there that Sabbath.

She was sitting in church, and Mrs. Gant, one of her friends, came up, hugged her, and squealed in delight. "What are you doing here at our church?"

"I came to see my son," Mom said proudly. "He's at the state college."

"Who is your son?"

He was sitting with several of his friends, and Mom pointed him out.

"*That's* your son?"

"He sure is, and his name is Fred."

"Then you must be proud of him. Do you know that boy comes to prayer meeting? He's the only really young person, but he's there every week. That's not all, honey. He's also here at nine o'clock every Sabbath morning."

Then Mrs. Gant said, "There's just one thing. As soon as the Sabbath service is over, I can't find him. We want to invite him home to eat with us, but he's always gone."

After the service, Mom asked Fred why he darted out so quickly.

"When I get out of church I run to the campus, trying to make it back in time for dinner," he said, "but I almost always miss it." He smiled and said, "But I have peanut butter and crackers, so I don't go hungry."

Mrs. Gant heard Fred's answer and was horrified. She grabbed his arm. "You'd better not run over to that campus anymore. You're going home with us."

"I was proud of Fred. I wasn't there to make him go to church, but the Bible says that if we train them up, they'll go the right way," Mom told the rest of us. "And 'train' means they have rules, regulations, and as parents we have to see that they adhere to them. It doesn't mean always whipping them to make sure they do it, but it means being good role models. Then when they're on their own, it's instilled in them and it will still be there."

It's true. What we learned at home plays out in our everyday actions, and often others remark on the ethical or kind behavior they see. It didn't start with us kids—it started at home with our parents.

Chapter 10

Families Take and Teach Worthy Work

Any honest job is good.

As part of our preparation for life, Mom assigned chores to each child in our family and she checked up to make sure we fulfilled those tasks. For instance, she taught each of us to wash and dry dishes. If we missed even one dish, she put everything back into the dishwater and made us do it again. I resented that the first time it happened to me, and I said, "But it looks clean."

"It may look clean to you, Larry, but that dish is not clean."

I was more than halfway through and wanted to hurry. Mom taught me a valuable lesson: If I did my job well the first time, I wouldn't have to do it again.

If we left the floor wet, didn't wipe off the cabinet, or did a poor job of washing clothes, Mom sent us back to start over. She expected excellence from us. Having a job in our home meant being responsible. Dad acted the same way when we worked outside in the yard. Whether it was raking leaves or cutting the grass, either we did it right or we kept on doing it until it was right.

Mom set a schedule every day. Every day each sibling had a task—for instance, wash dishes one day, clothes the next; clean the bathroom or mop the dining room floor, empty the trash, or wipe the kitchen counter. Nobody got extra, and no one got out of doing his or her share.

Deborah has this memory:

For as long as I can remember, we were required to make our beds as soon as we got up in the morning. We were taught that as we roll out of the bed, we roll up the covers. We were constantly bombarded with the statement "Do it right the first time and you won't have to do it over." I've heard other parents say this, but they failed to follow through to make doing it right the first time the more favorable option.

If Mom found wrinkles in our beds, she stripped them and we had to stay at it until she decided the beds were acceptable. After making the same bed three or four times, we realized the value of doing the job with excellence. In short, Mom taught all of us the value of diligence and thoroughness in the completion of a task.

As a child, I had a great deal of difficulty following through on the household chores. Mom called me a "pack rat," "junkyard dog," or a "clutter bug." She said, "I won't want to visit you as an adult, because the rats and roaches will run me out of the house." It seemed that no matter what I did, I just couldn't get into keeping things clean and neat. But Mom wouldn't let up on me. I did learn eventually.

It's amazing now that my home is probably the most well kept in the family. I can't stand things out of order. I'm constantly running the vacuum cleaner! When asked why I am so obsessed with household cleanliness, I remember my mother's prediction. I didn't want it to come true. I wanted Mom to come visit me.

In our family, we never had "boy chores" or "girl chores." Everyone washed dishes and learned to cook. My mother said, "I'm going to teach you boys too, because you might grow up and marry a woman who doesn't do a lot of cooking. Then you can take care of yourselves."

My dad was a good cook, and that probably influenced us. If he didn't mind cooking occasionally, why should I? He made the evening meal from time to time, and he also cooked breakfast on weekends. He especially liked to make special pancakes that he called "daddy cakes." They were really good.

Mom has often said, "In our house, everybody had a chance to learn how to do everything. Some of my friends didn't agree with me, but I didn't change."

"I don't allow my boys to wash dishes," they said, or "I don't allow my boys to wash clothes."

"That's girls' work," another said, "and I don't make my boys do that."

"No, that's not true," Mom replied. "That's everybody's work."

We had a few rules that went along with doing our daily work at home. One was whoever finds or makes a mess has to clean it up.

Today, as a physician, I sometimes go by the hospital to check on a child. If the diaper needs changing, I change it. Some doctors leave babies unwrapped, but I've always put their blankets back on and done whatever I could for the infant's comfort. If during a surgical procedure I drop something on the floor, when the surgery is over, instinctively I pick it up myself.

One time a nurse tried to stop me. "You're a doctor. You don't have to worry about that stuff."

"My mama said, 'If you make a mess, you clean it up,'" I answered. "This is just the way we do things."

Harrises are never above what others consider "menial" jobs. All work is honorable.

Although our parents laid down strict rules, they never directed any of us toward a particular career. The type of work we chose wasn't important; it was important that we did our best in our field. More than once we kids heard Mom say, "You can be a doctor or a lawyer or a teacher. Or you can be a garbage man, and even if you're a garbage man, be the best one you can."

Mitchell recalls Dad saying, "Be the best at whatever you're going to do in life. If you're going to be a bum, be the best bum. If you're going to be a doctor, be the best doctor. Whatever you do in life, strive for perfection."

We grew up with that attitude. Fred and I cut grass during our high school summers. When I came home from college for the summer, I worked as a janitor, and another time I washed dishes out at Fort Bragg.

The only time I ever remember anyone in the family rebelling was one summer when Deborah was also hired to work at Fort Bragg, in the mess hall's serving line. After the meal, the mess sergeant told her, "Get a bucket and water and mop the floor."

"I don't mop anybody's floor," she said.

"You mop it or you don't work here."

"Then I quit," she said.

That evening at the dinner table, Deborah told us what happened. I think she was a little proud of having stood up for herself.

"You know, it's an honor these days to work," Dad said quietly. "I don't care what you do. If it's honest, then it's not beneath you to do it."

She complained about how hard she had worked, that she was tired after standing for hours; then she told us the mean way the mess sergeant spoke to her. "Besides that, the mop is too big and it's heavy and—"

"That's not a problem. You mop floors at home. So tomorrow you can get a little mop and go back out there."

She didn't argue, but she still wasn't happy.

"Was anybody hurting you out there?"

"No, sir."

"Did anybody ask you to steal anything?"

"No, sir."

"Will you be getting paid?"

"Yes, sir."

"Then it sounds like you have an honest job. I don't see any reason why you can't go back and mop. Do you?"

The next day, Deborah apologized to the mess sergeant and was back on her job for the rest of the summer vacation.

I can think of two times when we were tested, once for Fred and once for me.

Fred finished dental school in May of 1976 with a D.D.S. from Howard University in Washington, D.C. He had been in the Army ROTC in college at A&T State University. The ROTC paid for his education, but it also obligated him to serve as a dentist in the army for two years.

He didn't have to report for induction until August. Like any of us would, Fred went out to find a temporary job. After trying a number of places and getting nothing, he went to the Pepsi-Cola plant where Mitchell had been hired for the summer. The company hired Fred as a Pepsi handler. That meant he had to collect glass bottles and load them into crates. Being a deliveryman, the lowest paying job and the hardest physically, wasn't easy. Back then, all the bottles were glass, and sometimes those bottles broke. Fred not only had to learn to carry heavy crates, but he had to clean up any broken glass as well as pick up and deliver.

On Fred's first trip back to the plant, the supervisor noticed he wore gloves. "Got cold hands?"

"No," Fred said and continued to unload crates.

"Then why you wearing gloves?"

"I'm a dentist. My skill depends on the condition of my hands, so I'm taking care of them."

The supervisor laughed, but that didn't matter. Fred continued to wear his gloves in hundred-degree temperatures. Frequently when he pulled into the plant and the supervisor saw him, Fred faced ridicule.

"You know why he's wearing those nice gloves?" the supervisor yelled to anyone around. "It's because he's a dentist, that's why!" Then he laughed, because apparently it struck him as funny. (Later this supervisor became one of Fred's dental patients.)

"What's a dentist doing in this place?" someone asked him.

"Just what I'm being paid to do," Fred said. He didn't stop to talk. Although Fred told us about the incident, he never looked on his job as anything he was too good for. He told me, "Larry, I'm going to be the best deliveryman they have."

Dad had taught us well. He said that if we saw a job opportunity, go after it, and if it was the only thing available, "Don't be ashamed—it's an honest living."

The other test involved me. Before I graduated from Yale, the medical school at Duke University accepted me to enter in the fall of 1973. I wanted a job that summer. In fact, it wouldn't have occurred to any of us not to work during our summers off from school. We'd been doing it since we were kids. It just seemed natural.

When I searched for a job, the youth employment counselor, who was White, interviewed me. I explained that I had finished Yale and was going to medical school to become a doctor.

"I have the perfect position for you," she said. "It's at the medical clinic at Pope Air Force Base."

I assumed that I would be working inside and would have some exposure to patient care. When I arrived on the scene, I wore a tie and dress shirt. I should have caught on when the personnel director stared at the way I was dressed.

"You are the gardener," he said. The only exposure I would experience was to the hot sun. The personnel director sent me outside as the new cleanup man.

I smiled at that, thinking I had had plenty of experience mowing lawns. The woman from the youth employment office knew what the job was when she interviewed me. I knew that the clinic had a clerk position open, and two of us arrived that day. I had assumed that would be my position. I had learned to type and was good at it. The poor woman might have typed twenty words a minute. I was a Black male and she was a White female. I became the gardener, and she became clerk/typist.

I didn't complain. I was grateful to have a job, and I determined to show everyone the cleanest yard on the base.

When I got home that first evening, my clothes were so perspiration-soaked that they looked as if I had been caught in the rain. That didn't concern me. They would wash.

All summer I dedicated myself to being the best outside man they had ever hired. I kept my area clean and the grass clipped. Although disappointed, and aware that my being outside was a racial issue, I refused to allow that to interfere with my level of commitment. No one tried any harder around there than I did. After all, I had a job, and Dad had constantly reminded us that all honest work is good. I had summer employment, and I could make some money. I took pride in that opportunity and in knowing that my yard would impress anyone who visited.

Within a few days of being hired, I met people who staffed the clinic. Once they learned I was a future physician, they invited me in to use their library anytime I wanted. Sometimes after work, I went in and studied for an hour.

Working hard at a distasteful job wasn't just something that happened back in my early years. I feel exactly the same way today. I'm now a medical doctor, a practicing pediatrician, and I started my own clinic in 1980. I still believe no job is too small or beneath my dignity. For example, a few weeks ago, one of the commodes in the clinic overflowed. I got out the plunger and took care of it, then grabbed a mop and began to clean the floor.

Just then, the mother of one of my patients walked down the hallway. She almost passed by me and then stopped. "Uh, Dr. Harris?"

"Yes," I said and paused from my mopping.

"You—you are Dr. Harris?"

"That's right." I went back to mopping.

"What are you doing, mopping the floor?"

"Who else is going to mop it?" I kept on.

Just then two other mothers came in and she yelled, "Look, that's Dr. Harris, and he's mopping the floor! Can you believe that?"

"I mop floors if they need it," I said, "and it's because my mama always said, 'If you find a mess, you clean it up.' I found a mess, and I'm doing just what she said."

They laughed, and I overheard one of them say she wished her husband had been trained that way.

Until the mother acted surprised, it hadn't occurred to me that I was doing anything unusual. I was just following training that I had received more than forty years earlier.

By contrast, I want to tell you about a relative of mine. He finished college and couldn't find a job right away. I said something to him about applying at a fast-food place.

"I refuse to work at Hardees; I refuse to work at McDonald's."

"But why? It's not big money, but it's—"

"I'm too educated to do that kind of thing," he said.

I didn't argue with him, but I felt sorry for him.

That evening I told my two children, Michelle and Larry Jr., about what had happened. I smiled as I realized that I was beginning to sound exactly like my father. And frankly, I liked that. "If for some reason I couldn't be a physician and I had to go out and cut grass to pay the bills," I told them, "I wouldn't have any problem with that." I started telling them about their grandfather. Yes, I knew they had heard it all their lives, but I wanted to tell them again.

My two kids listened as I told them about all the part-time jobs my father did, and I hoped they enjoyed hearing about their grandfather as much as I enjoyed talking about my number one hero.

As I talked, of course, I told them about the jobs Fred and I had taken after we finished college. Then I thought about Mike, one of the twins, when he was home for the summer after his first year of college. The only employment he could find was the dirty, hard job of standing on the back of a truck and collecting garbage. He didn't complain.

"Larry, I'm the best garbage collector in the city." His attitude reminded me of high school days when he boasted, "I'm the smartest in the family."

You see, my dad realized that we need to find pride not in our position, but rather in the work we do in that position—whatever it is.

Our work ethic started at home.

Chapter 11

The Best Classroom
Is the Living Room

Set goals and achieve them.

D on't follow the pack," Dad urged.

"You've got to stand for something," Mom loved to say. "If you don't stand for something, you'll fall for anything."

Those words became important to us.

One thing all of us remember is that our parents never pushed us to come home with straight A's or to achieve more than we were able. "Do your best" was what we heard.

We became quite competitive among ourselves. Each of us tried to bring home better grades than the others.

Did it work? Deborah, Michael, Mabel, and I were high school and junior high student body presidents; Michael and I were high school valedictorians; Deborah, Michael, Mitchell, Freda, Ruth, and Mabel were all youth leaders of the church on the state level. I'm a church elder. Deborah has held national leadership positions in her church.

Yes, it worked.

All of us thrived on academic competition—Michael and I probably the most. He always thought he was smarter than I was. Of course, I knew he was mistaken. We loved to tease each other. "Don't mess with me," I told him regularly, "because I am the best."

He only laughed, because he was convinced he was intellectually superior.

Our parents didn't mind that kind of friendly competition. If Michael ever received a grade higher than I did (and I can't remember that happening), I would have been as happy for him as if it had been my own.

Our parents were really good about this. Dad constantly said, "Do your best. You don't always have to make A's. If C is your best, then proudly bring home a C."

It's strange, but that freedom made me try even harder.

Once Fred and I started high school, we developed an odd sleeping pattern. Every school night we went to bed at ten o'clock and slept for five hours. Both of us got up, studied for an hour or maybe two, and then we went back to sleep for another hour. At six o'clock all of us were up, getting ready for the day.

Mom wasn't troubled, and she didn't complain about our not getting enough sleep. "If my boys got sleepy, I knew they'd sleep," she said years later.

When we brought home report cards, we showed them to our parents. I found it interesting to watch them read the cards. Dad read the left-hand side of the page that showed our grades. He commented and always encouraged us if we had earned good grades or if we had improved since the previous period.

When Mom picked up the cards, she immediately scrutinized the right-hand page, which was the place for grades on our behavior. We knew it was harder to please Mom than it was Dad.

One time, Mabel received a C in conduct, although everything else on her report card was A's and B's. Mom warned her, "You're my daughter. You will never again come home with a C in conduct."

"Yes, ma'am," she answered.

Mabel never did.

Twice the twins, Mitch and Mike, had C's in conduct. The second time they began to cry.

"Why are you crying?" asked another student. "You got A's and B's."

"Because we got a C in conduct, and Mama's going to beat us."

They knew what to expect. Mom knew both of them liked to talk in class. She spanked them both times. But she spanked them only twice. They never made C's in conduct again.

Mom taught us very early, "Your reputation is all that you have even when you're gone. Your reputation will follow you wherever you go." She used to say, "If I see your teacher in the grocery store and she tells me you're doing well with your grades but not well with your behavior, then that's not good enough."

We loved it, of course, when she'd say something like this: "Larry, I saw your teacher in the store today, and she said you are behaving in school. That's good. That's exactly what I expected to hear."

Fred never made top grades. They were good, B's and C's, but he could have done better. Dad kept saying, "Fred, you can improve."

We used to call him Hoppergrass—meaning that Dad laughingly called him a grasshopper that just kept jumping around in the grass. That name fit Fred, because he didn't seem to want to settle down and study hard like the rest of us. "Well, maybe he's not as smart as Larry is," my mother said. "Just leave him alone. He can get a good trade when he finishes school."

"No, the boy can do better work." Dad stayed right on him.

The real change in his attitude happened the summer after Fred finished tenth grade. He landed a job with the Youth Corps. The group he worked with kept the city streets clean by picking up trash and getting rid of weeds in public places.

The work that summer was a powerful time of insight for Fred. He said to me, "If I don't get my grades up, I might be doing this the rest of my life." One night at dinner he said to all of us, "There's no way I'm going to do this kind of work after I get out of school."

He meant it and he changed. As soon as he finished high school, he enrolled in college and went to dental school. After his first year, his grades had changed from B's and C's to A's and B's.

"I told you," Dad said to Mom. "I told you that boy could do it."

Except for Fred, the rest of us were pretty aggressive in our studies. Deborah—who now holds a Ph.D.—was a good student, but she wasn't one of the better students in the household. She holds one unique honor: She's the only nonmember of the Honor Society who became president of the student body. Her grades weren't quite high enough to be in the Honor Society. Of course, we teased her about it, but no one gets past Deborah.

"You don't have to be a genius to be the president," she said.

Even though Deborah and I were both student body presidents at our high school, she was better at it than I had been. She was more assertive and implemented a lot of things that the students wanted.

One reason she wasn't the best student in the family was because she was energetic and always involved in many activities. Even while she was in high school, Deborah did a lot of public speaking at church and school functions. Of the nine of us, she is the most verbal and just a natural at speaking to crowds.

After Deborah, Mabel and Michael were also class or student body president. A teacher told our mother, "You Harrises have started a dynasty at E. E. Smith High School."

Mom and Dad were involved in more than our grades and school behavior. When we lived in Germany, Mom once went to the zoo three times in one week because Fred, Deborah, and I were in different classes and we all had field trips there. When our teacher asked for parents to volunteer to go with us, all three of us assured them that Mom would go. It never occurred to any of us not to volunteer Mom. I'm sure it never occurred to Mom not to go.

Mom attended all our school events. That meant she spent a lot of her time at our activities, because there were nine of us. Somehow she sat in the stands at every football, baseball, and basketball game and showed up for all our school plays and PTA meetings. Dad came to everything unless he was in the field (on military duty).

Sometimes Fred and I played on opposite teams, and several times we played against each other. That didn't matter to our parents: They rooted for both of us. Once, when I had just gotten on base and Fred was catching, I was playing off the bag and he threw me out—and I couldn't live that down. Mom still cheered for both of us.

Even after she began to work, if one of us was involved in an important school event, Mom asked for time off. Because she worked hard and conscientiously, and put in extra hours, they never minded when she asked for two hours to go to a school play.

We knew that Mom would be there for everything at school that was important to us. As much as anything else, that told us how much our parents cared about us. Her presence also made our teachers aware of her deep commitment to our education, especially at those times when she was the only parent who could attend scheduled events.

As I said, Mom went to all of our ball games, and she hasn't stopped. She still attends when any of the grandchildren play. I doubt that she's ever missed a game.

I learned that lesson well. When my son, Larry Jr., was in high school, I sometimes closed my office early or rescheduled appointments so I wouldn't have to miss a game. They called me "Larry, the team dad." I was the one father who attended every game.

Here's where I saw my parents at their best. My graduation ceremony from Yale University in New Haven, Connecticut, was at eleven o'clock on a Monday morning in June of 1973. Michael and Mitchell were graduating from E. E. Smith High School in Fayetteville, North Carolina, that same day at five o'clock. My parents figured out how to attend both ceremonies. Along with Fred and his wife, Karen, they

Fred and Ruth Harris didn't just tell their children to make goals and achieve them—they did so themselves. Fred earned his BA in Business Administration from Shaw University at age 53, and after raising nine children Ruth worked as a teacher's aide nurturing hundreds of other kids.

drove to New Haven. Fred and Karen were going to collect my stuff and drive back the next day. Fred would take my parents to the airport after my graduation so they could fly to Fayetteville. Because there was no direct flight, they would have to change planes in Washington, D.C.

The first leg of the flight went well; however, a severe thunderstorm delayed their takeoff from Washington, D.C., for an hour and a half.

Michael was the high school valedictorian, and that made it even more important for them to get back for the graduation and hear their son make his speech. When they rushed into the auditorium, though, the ceremony was almost over. Michael had finished his speech, and they didn't get to hear him.

It was, of course, a big disappointment to them, but I don't think Michael minded. What impressed him and the rest of us was the trouble they went to just to get to both places. The attempt to attend both graduations didn't surprise any of us. It was typical behavior for Mom and Dad.

While we were young, I remember Dad saying to us that he expected all of us to go to college but that he couldn't afford to send us. He told us that we were going to have to get academic scholarships. That was his goal for each of us. He instilled in us the value of determination. He constantly reminded us of what our lives would be like without a good education. Dad never let us become satisfied with being average when he knew we could do better. He just kept pushing us until we achieved to the level where he knew we were doing our best.

Dad reminded us that hard work never killed anyone. He taught us how to overcome obstacles by sharing the obstacles in his life. He taught us how to accomplish many things. "Don't think about it; just do it," he'd say.

Deborah says,

> Another thing we learned was how to plan strategically so that we could accomplish our goals. By example and endless illustrations, Dad taught us to bounce back when we had fallen. Right along with that, we learned that if one of us fell, the others were to help pick him or her up. When we felt discouraged or downhearted, Dad affectionately, but seriously, reminded us that a real soldier doesn't run away when the battle gets tough. I constantly found myself trying to be a good soldier. That little statement has caused me to overcome impossible circumstances in order to achieve as a single parent of two children.

When college time came for me, I had finished my senior year in high school with the highest grade point average in my class. That opened up a variety of scholarship offers. I had planned to stay in North Carolina. Fred was at a Black college, A&T State University in Greensboro, North Carolina. I thought of enrolling there as well, but I also considered the University of North Carolina at Chapel Hill, Duke University, Wake Forest, and Yale.

A race riot had broken out at A&T during Fred's first year, and the National Guard killed one student, so I decided not to go there. At Duke, Black students had recently taken over one of the university buildings. Wake Forest, the University of North Carolina, and Yale University had all sent me letters of acceptance. The previous year another student from our school was accepted at Yale, and he tried to recruit me. Not only was Yale among the most prestigious universities in the nation, but it also offered the best scholarships.

My only hesitancy about Yale was that it was so far away, and I knew my mother really wanted me to go to Wake Forest in Winston-Salem, North Carolina, because it was fairly close. Whenever I brought up the subject, however, Mom said, "It's your choice, Larry. You have to make that decision. Whatever you decide will be the right choice."

I asked Dad, hoping he would tell me which school to choose. "It's up to you, son."

After a lot of prayer and thought, I chose Yale.

That fall I boarded a Trailways bus and rode for fourteen hours, but it seemed like longer. On that bus, more than once I asked myself, *Have I lost my mind?*

After I entered Yale, I experienced culture shock. Not only was it a prestigious university, but also a lot of wealthy and famous people, such as Sheila Firestone Ford and Sara Pillsbury, went there. I soon realized that my classmates were sons of top Wall Street stock brokers and international lawyers. More than that, I met some of the smartest people in my life. I had done well on my SAT scores, but one of the first students I met had earned a perfect score. I had always thought I was bright, but I soon learned that everyone in class was bright.

Shortly after I started meeting other students, I learned that one of the first questions they asked each other was "What kind of work does your father do?" A famous lawyer's son was the first to ask me.

"Oh, he's in the army," I said, and I didn't think anything more about it.

The next day, the lawyer's son said, "I was talking to my father yesterday and mentioned you. He said he had heard of a Black general named Harris. Is that your dad?"

"That's not my dad. He's a sergeant."

My roommate seemed embarrassed, but I wasn't. My dad had taught us to have pride in our family, regardless of what they did for a living.

My dad's being a sergeant didn't affect my grades, and the people who liked me liked me for myself anyway. I never apologized for my background. Why should I? In fact, I was proud of it.

I really struggled at Yale—it was the hardest I ever had to work in my entire academic career. I thought the first English paper I wrote was excellent.

When the instructor, Etta Onot, returned the paper, I read these words across the top: "I cannot grade this; I need to see you in conference."

She meant it was really bad. My heart sank. I had worked hard, and I thought I had known what I was doing.

Professor Onot told me, "I want to help you." We sat down at her desk, and she went through the paper sentence by sentence, telling me everything I had done wrong.

I wondered how I had ever considered myself smart. If I was that bad, how could I have been the class valedictorian in high school?

"I want to help you because you have potential. The mechanics are good, but it's not well thought out." She said that I needed to be more analytical.

She spent several sessions working with me, teaching me how to write better papers. She even assigned a graduate student to help me. I felt grateful. I thanked God for such a fine teacher. Most of the professors at Yale were like that. That's when I knew I had made the right decision to accept a scholarship to Yale.

During my college days, the family remained supportive. I didn't have much money, so I ate at the cafeteria. That meant my meals were all paid in advance. Food wasn't a problem, but I didn't have any spending money. When I wanted to go home at Christmas or during the summer, my parents had to send funds.

As I mentioned earlier, the first time I went to Yale I rode the bus from Fayetteville to New Haven. I was very naive. I had a huge trunk, and when I got there, I had to take a cab from the station to the campus.

"You can't put that in my car," the driver said.

"I'm not going to leave it here."

"Then you'll have to walk."

That's exactly what I did. I studied the map so that I knew where to go, and I started out. I think it was about two miles, so I walked the entire distance, dragging my trunk with me. Later Dad said, "You should have told the driver you'd pay him extra if he put that in the cab. He would have done it." As a part-time cab driver, Dad knew how the system worked. I was so inexperienced that I didn't think of such a thing. It was the first time I had ever tried to take a cab anyplace.

Years later I teased my parents, "I guess you don't like me as much as the other kids. All of us went to college, but you drove all of them to their schools. I had to take the bus."

Of course, Dad pointed out that I had chosen to go to a school six hundred miles away and the others went to schools in North Carolina.

In fact, I've often wondered if my parents didn't want me to go to Yale. They never said that and never spoke a word against my decision. I do know that I had to be at the bus station in Fayetteville to catch a bus that left at one o'clock in the morning. Fred drove me. That was another thing I teased my parents about.

We have earned our way. Nothing has been handed to us. Mom and Dad taught us that important principle early in life.

I made my way at Yale through hard work, loving support from my family, and a caring group of Christians at our church.

But I think most of my strength came from Mom and Dad's encouragement to do my best, to aim high, and to work relentlessly toward my goal. Every one of us took their challenge.

Chapter 12

Family Gives You
a Reason
to Press On

In the face of failure and disappointment, drive on.

One of the things I love most about Dad is the way he taught us to handle heartache and disappointment. When things didn't go the way we wanted, Dad pleaded with us not to be bitter. "Don't fight what you can't change. Just go on with your life. Just drive on."

"Just drive on." I wonder how many times I heard Dad say that. It was certainly his motto for living. More than once I've repeated that motto and found comfort in it. Bitterness, anger, and resentment—not one of those things is good for us. They only hurt us, as Dad often said. Instead, we just drive on.

This became one of the most valuable lessons the Harris children ever learned. I don't want to give the impression that just because we had wise and caring parents, our lives went smoothly for us. Like all people do, each of us faced many disappointments in life.

In the previous chapter, I said I entered Yale. Before that I had never brought home a single grade below a B. My first year at Yale, I earned only average marks. Then I failed physics during the first semester of my sophomore year. That was a devastating blow. A very discouraged young man called home and said, "I'm ready to quit." I felt that I had decreased my chances of getting into medical school.

"You can't do that, son," Dad said, and Mom echoed him. "You just drive on and take the course again."

I did, and I passed it the second time. Once past my disappointment at failing a class, I felt challenged to study harder. During my senior year I had all honors. The culture-shocked country boy from North Carolina proved that he was truly the son of Fred and Ruth Harris.

I had planned to return to North Carolina for medical school. After my training as a pediatrician, I wanted to set up a practice in my hometown, Fayetteville. I would then become the first Black pediatrician in the city.

First came medical school. I had applied to several medical schools in North Carolina—Duke, Bowman Gray, and the University of North Carolina. All of them accepted me. After a few days of intense thinking, praying, and talking with my siblings and my church friends, I decided on Duke.

Our joint family plan was to start the Harris Medical Clinic in Fayetteville, with Fred the dentist and Larry the pediatrician. One of the twins planned to be a pediatrician, the other, an obstetrician. And about that time, Dad retired from the military and went to college to work toward his degree in business administration. He would become our business manager in the clinic. Everything seemed to be going just right for us. We were not only best friends, but we would be colleagues in business together.

After the twins earned their bachelor's degrees, they applied to medical school and weren't accepted. That's when the family dream died. It was probably the single biggest family disappointment for us boys and for Dad as well. The idea had been solid. We knew we could make it happen if we had the opportunity. We also had to admit that we couldn't control all the forces of life.

The twins' grades were certainly high enough, but they didn't make it past the interview process, which is the last big step. They never learned the reason.

That was a harsh blow, especially for Michael, who was such a high achiever. He felt defeated because he had failed at his goal to become a physician. It wasn't his fault, but he still saw it as failure.

"Let's drive on, boys," Dad said. I think he said it with more bravado than he felt, because I know this was just as devastating for him. Dad, as usual, wouldn't dwell on what couldn't be.

Despite their disappointments, the twins knew Dad was right—they had to move on. They heard about job opportunities with a local pharmaceutical company. They applied and both began to work there in 1977. The twins could have reapplied to medical school the following year, but they liked their positions with the pharmaceutical company so well that they chose to keep working instead.

Michael and Mitchell became the first Black sales representatives in the Southeast for their company. Mitchell is currently regional sales manager and lives in metro-Atlanta; Michael is district sales manager and operates out of Durham, North Carolina. Because of the minority glass ceiling, however, they aren't as far along in their careers as they expected. It's been discouraging to them—and others—that year after year they have been the top sales leaders in their respective areas and yet people with lower achievement levels have passed them by. Both of my brothers have trained White salespeople who have had less time with the company and lower rates of success, but who became directors in the corporation.

Of course, it hurts—and it hurts me as their older brother who has to see this from afar. But then I get more angry about it than they do. They're not bitter.

In fact, while a number of other Blacks have been passed over and moved on to other companies to enter into higher positions, my brothers keep driving on. They don't talk about it often, but they see themselves as role models. They feel they have to pave the way for younger Blacks and other minorities in the industry and to encourage them to keep on trying.

Like Dad, they don't quit because of injustice. They just try harder.

Yes, all of us suffered from the disappointment of the clinic never becoming a reality. Again, we heeded Dad's wisdom. "If plan A doesn't work, we go to plan B."

That's what we did.

I've mentioned that in 1988 I faced the lowest moment of my life: I developed a brain tumor. Because of its location, we didn't know if I would survive, become incapacitated, be blind, or die.

Only days earlier, Bertie and I had had the foundation laid for our dream house. I was ready to stop the building and back out of everything. I expected Dad to support that. He was the logical businessman.

"Drive on; don't stop," Dad said.

"No, this is your house," Mom said. "You've dreamed and planned for it."

I felt encouraged. I also remembered that even as a little kid, when my parents set a goal, they never quit. I was only thirty-eight years old, but I thought my life was over. My wife and my family wouldn't allow me to think like that. My siblings also reminded me that I wasn't to worry about Bertie or my children.

"We'll take care of them if anything happens to you," Fred promised.

The surgery was successful. We didn't need plan B.

Deborah faced heavy disappointments when she was a student at the University of North Carolina at Chapel Hill, where she had already earned a master of education. She began to work on her Ph.D. two years later. That in itself was an ordeal, but about that time she and her husband separated.

She tells how she faced a big choice. "Should I remain with my husband of eleven years, or should I leave him to ensure the safety of my children?" she wondered. Her marriage had always been troubled and rocky. She stayed married because in our family she learned this: "We don't quit. We do everything we can to achieve our goals." Later, though, Deborah realized she wasn't listening to the other thing Dad used to say—that holding on isn't always the right thing to do, that there are times you need to drive on and learn to make the best out of a bad situation.

Deborah admits,

> In retrospect, I realize that to remain in such an unhealthy situation had nothing to do with remaining strong. While I was going through my ordeal, I kept thinking that we could work out the differences. Of course, as a responsible adult, and with the background I came from, for a long time I assumed I had failed, and I thought I could figure out how to fix the situation. I kept thinking of my parents and their

wonderful marriage. Why couldn't mine be as good as theirs? At least, why couldn't I have a solid, stable one? My siblings had good marriages, so what was wrong with me?

In time I realized that I was doing everything I knew to make ours a happy relationship. What brought me to the deciding point was when I faced the reality that our children's lives and futures were involved in this bad relationship. My parents taught us, by example and words, that nothing or no one was more important than our children. What kind of example were my husband and I setting for them?

Our mom often said, "Children are innocent. They didn't ask to be born, so you give them all you have. Forget about yourself and make sure the children are okay. They are the future."

Those words stayed with Deborah. She says now, "Mom was right, and that's how I slowly came to make what I believe was the right choice."

Dad was right too. He taught us that sometimes we have to sacrifice the comforts of life to take advantage of greater opportunities. That's what Deborah chose. Every day she traveled a total of two hours round trip from Greensboro to Chapel Hill to pursue her doctorate. It was in Greensboro that she and her husband had accepted a joint position as live-in night caretakers in a home for the elderly. This provided free rent, utilities, food, and a small salary. It was quite a step backward from the new home they had owned and Deborah's steady, good-paying job. She had to start over financially while she continued her education.

"As I look back, I wonder how I held up during that three-year period," she says now, then adds, "It seems obvious now that the biggest single reason was the backing and love of my parents and siblings.

"When I hit low spots—and I hit many of them—my family came through every time. My mother quickly reminded me: 'Honey, God is in control, and all things are possible through God.' Just to hear her say those words with such true conviction was enough to lift me out of my black hole."

So eventually Deborah and her husband divorced. She explains, "I sucked up my disappointments and unhappiness and did what I could to make certain my children didn't suffer. Plan A had failed. It was time for plan B."

Deborah moved home and will never forget that moment she drove into our parents' driveway.

"I felt broken and devastated," she says. "I thought I had let down the family, God, and myself. As I got out of the car, my legs felt weak and I didn't know if I had the strength to say anything. I felt confident that none of my family members knew what I had been going through, but I didn't want to recount all of the pain then. I just wanted someone to understand without my having to say anything. My mother met me with open arms. She hugged me and held me tight. The tears flowed, and I couldn't hold them back. 'I'm sorry—I—I just couldn't stay—'"

"You took more than I would have taken," Mother whispered in her ear. "You don't have anything to be ashamed of. Hold your head up and drive on."

"You know what I've been going through?" Deborah sobbed. "How could you know? I've been careful to conceal everything."

Our mother hugged her again and said, "Don't you think I know when my child is not happy? Of course I know."

"Those words flowed through me," Deborah says. "She was my mother and she knew. Without my ever having to say anything, she felt my pain. I wept and she held me as if I were a ten-year-old child again. The comfort of those arms made me know my life was going to be all right."

From that day forward, Deborah realized the power of having parental support no matter the circumstances. She had married against our father's recommendations and against her brothers' admonition. But her family didn't care about being right. They cared that one of their own was hurting, and they did everything they could to support her.

"Only then did I realize that my parents sensed a great deal about what I had gone through, but they never interfered or encouraged me to leave," Deborah says. "Instead, they encouraged patience, understanding, and working things through as long as I wanted to stay married. The moment I chose to end the marriage, however, they supported me, accepted my decision, and encouraged me for having the strength to make that choice. The entire family propped me up as I began to live the new, single parent life."

Single parenting wasn't easy. One of Deborah's greatest challenges was needing to function as two parents. She tried to become everything to her children: the nurturer, disciplinarian, spiritual leader, teacher, nurse, playmate, counselor, provider, cook, cleaner, and whatever else they needed.

Another huge challenge was finances. As an independent person, Deborah grew weary of always being on the begging end. "My attitude was wrong," she says now, "and I was filled with pride—too proud to ask."

Fred reminded her that if the situation were reversed, she would have done everything she could for any member of the family.

Deborah knew that, but she still hesitated to ask. "I'm just tired of begging," she said.

Fred humbled her: "We're not tired of giving."

On each occasion when the family learned Deborah had a need, they chastised her as they once again practiced our family philosophy: Family first. If one of us is in need, all of us respond. We take care of each other, because family is all we have.

Fred became her closest confidant. He regularly sent her cards and little trinkets to encourage her. "I remember wishing I could just have a conversation with my big brother without crying or moaning over my latest problem," Deborah recalls.

At that time, Fred was having his own financial problems and almost lost his dental practice. Yet his situation didn't stop him from doing what he could. He gave his total heart in support. Fred was calm and reflective, a man not easily ruffled. His constancy regularly reminded Deborah of how God interacts patiently with us. It didn't matter how often she cried or the number of times she complained, Fred always listened. "He helped me see more fully the reality of a caring, compassionate God," Deborah says.

She adds,

> By contrast, Larry didn't possess the calmness of Fred, but he was a financial genius and seemed to know how to bail me out of one money problem after another. I became so tired of asking for financial assistance that I let the utility company turn off our lights rather than ask for help again. My two children, Eugene and Tonya, and I slept on the floor because I couldn't afford to buy beds. I was so weary, and I didn't want to need anyone else.

When my siblings learned that we had been sleeping on the floor and that our electricity had been off for three days, they were annoyed with me. I heard some of the strongest words of anger from Larry and the others over that. When they discovered that we didn't have anything to eat in my apartment, they were even more exasperated with me.

After being chastened many times for not asking, Deborah gave in and began to ask when she needed help. Another challenge cropped up.

"Once I began to ask," she explains, "I seemed caught in a trap of not being able to do anything for myself. I began to lean on my siblings. I became too dependent. Larry then taught me a hard but life-changing lesson."

He and Bertie had done a lot to help me financially, but without realizing it, I had become complacent with that assistance and had begun to expect support from him. That was just as wrong as letting my pride refuse their help.

One time I went to Larry and asked for money.

"No," he said.

I stared at him, unable to believe what I had just heard. "But—but you've always—"

"You've become dependent on Bertie and me. That's not good for you." He said more than that and I cried, but even as he spoke, I knew he was right. I had learned to rely on others, and I wasn't doing everything I could to help myself. I haven't asked for financial support from any of my family members since. Larry's refusal was exactly the jolt I needed, even though it was painful to have to hear it. Because while his words and attitude hurt me, they also healed me and kept me from falling into a pattern of helplessness. Larry was not only my older brother, but also a true friend. He helped me learn anew what our parents taught us: that God helps those who help themselves, and that we shouldn't expect anyone to do something for us that we can do for ourselves. Our family members really can be our best friends.

Though Deborah found personal encouragement from the family, the odds had stacked against her finishing her doctoral program. Often, during the data entry and analysis part of her dissertation, she had to take her son and daughter with her to the research lab. They often would sleep alongside Deborah while she worked. At times, Eugene, who was eight years old, woke up and assisted her by calling out data, entering data, or just double-checking. It was clear that they knew at that young age the family philosophy: one in need—all respond—and all take care of each other because family is all you have.

Still, her advisor suggested, "Come back and finish when your life is more stable and your kids have grown."

"No, I'm going to finish now," she said.

She forced herself to be confident and determined to compete with the best of them.

She successfully competed for a federally funded student-initiated grant, completed her classes, did her oral exams, and received her doctoral degree before anyone in her class.

Where the program took the average doctoral candidate four years to complete, Deborah did it in three—and while living in campus housing, working part-time, and raising her two children. That's typical of my amazing sister. Yes, she earned her Ph.D., and I'm as proud of her as if I had earned it myself.

Today she's a professor in the field of special education at the University of South Florida at Tampa, and she's also a well-known motivational speaker.

Other family members faced daunting circumstances. Although I had the brain tumor, Michael's physical problems have been equally severe. I've mentioned that he's diabetic, and one serious side effect is kidney failure. In 1991 he went on dialysis. I don't think most people would have held on and fought the way Michael did. I never heard him complain or feel sorry for himself. He always insisted that God was with him and was giving him the strength.

During the nearly ten years he remained on dialysis, he worked full time. I don't know how he did it, because dialysis takes three or four hours, two to three times a week. In his work he usually traveled four or five times a week to various states around the country such as Missouri, Alabama, California, Georgia, Florida, North Carolina, South Carolina, and Virginia. When he was due for dialysis, he had to make arrangements in the many different cities where he traveled.

One time, he told me that he had made arrangements for dialysis during a sales meeting in Hawaii. At the last minute, the staff at the facility in Honolulu decided they couldn't do the procedure. Rather than argue with them, Mike immediately booked a flight to Los Angeles. Within two hours of his arrival, he began his treatment. That evening he was on the plane again, returning to Honolulu to finish the sales meetings.

It's also important to point out that despite Mike's serious problem, his district stayed at the top in sales for the corporation. Nothing made him let up or gave him an excuse for doing less than his best for the company.

"Why don't you slow down?" I once asked him. I also suggested he take a medical retirement.

I should have known better. He was our parents' son, and he kept that determination to drive on in spite of the worst physical disabilities. "Drive on" was every Harris child's motto, and we always had a plan B. It started at home.

Chapter 13

You Learn Integrity at Home

Pay back what you borrow or it's stealing.

Some people might think that because we were a large family and my dad didn't make a large income, we grew up deprived, or at least feeling poor or underprivileged. None of my siblings or I felt that way.

It's one of the most valuable lessons we learned in childhood, even though none of us would have been able to articulate it until we had our own families: When children know they are loved, their possessions aren't very important.

That doesn't mean money didn't matter. It did, and our parents managed a small income very carefully. Yet having things or not having them never became an issue.

One of the lessons Dad wanted us to understand was the value of a dollar. Other than Mabel, who remained the family housekeeper, the rest of us worked outside the home as soon as we were able to get part-time jobs. We were also taught to be responsible with our money.

The first lesson Dad taught us, however, seemed unjust, and it was one of the few times I remember being angry with him. Fred and I had just entered our teens and had begun to cut lawns to earn money.

Dad sharpened the blades of the lawnmower, and we prepared to go out. "Just one thing," he said. "Half of what you make you turn over to me."

"Half?" I asked in disbelief.

"Then we won't have much left," Fred said. "The church gets 10 percent off the total amount. If you get 50 percent after that, it sure doesn't leave much for us."

"Why do you want half our money?" I asked.

"That half is for your room and board."

"You're our father," Fred said quietly. "We shouldn't have to pay room and board."

"You're living here, aren't you? You're eating, aren't you? If I don't pay for it, you have to pay for it."

We went out about eight o'clock in the morning, and by noon we'd made twelve dollars, which was a lot of money back in those days. We always split everything equally.

At the end of the first day, we put aside 10 percent for God, then we split the rest in half and put aside Dad's share. That left us with a total of five dollars and forty cents between us.

We were so excited about having our own money that it seemed like a fortune. We each took our portion of the remaining money and went to McCrory's—which is much like Kmart or Target. Fred spent his money on orange slices, and I bought M&Ms. We began eating our profits on the way back to the house.

Dad was already home by the time we got there. I rushed ahead and started telling him what a wonderful day we had. I'm sure he saw my mouth full of M&Ms.

"What did you do with the money?"

Fred explained how we divided it up and then handed Dad five dollars and forty cents. "Look what we bought," Fred said as he offered Dad a piece of orange candy.

Dad looked at us for a few seconds. "Okay, boys, let me have that candy."

Fred and I stared at each other while Dad called the other kids. "Come on out and see what your brothers brought home." He distributed every piece of candy to the other kids. He didn't give Fred or me another piece.

"Boys, you did good by going out and hustling and making some money, but you did bad by spending it on junk and only on yourselves." That's all he said and then he walked away.

"That's not fair," I said. "Fred and I made that money, and we should be able to do what we want with it."

Dad stopped and turned around. "To a certain extent that's true, but you were wasting it. You should save your money to buy things like clothes or schoolbooks—something worthwhile. One candy bar, that's all right, but you don't want to waste all your money."

"It's still not fair."

"You worked hard, but you don't work just for yourselves. That's why I took away your candy and gave it to your brothers and sisters."

I didn't say anything more. I stood there, realizing that our profits were all gone.

The next time we went out, we figured we'd make Daddy happy. We went to one of those cheap stores and each bought ourselves a shirt.

"See, Daddy," we said at home, "we bought shirts this time."

He looked them over and said, "That's okay, boys. At least you made an effort."

Yes, the shirts were cheap—so much so they faded the first time we washed them. We didn't realize that would happen, but Daddy could see what we had bought.

Mom didn't say anything then. When we took them out of the washer and they had faded, she said, "Now you have learned something. That's why you don't buy cheap stuff. You need to buy something that is going to last."

It was a difficult lesson, but both of us realized how we had wasted our money a second time. We never wasted it again.

Because money was scarce, we didn't have as many clothes as a lot of kids, but we had enough. Being the two oldest boys and almost the same size, Fred and I always got new clothes. Then we passed our things down to the twins and often down to Dyfierd as well.

When Mom bought us clothes they seemed to last forever. It was also interesting the way Mom made us dress. Each of us had a pair of shoes for church and a pair we wore for school and play. We were also responsible to keep our shoes polished and our clothes hung up. We did many things together but this was a totally individual matter: We were always mindful of taking care of our own needs.

The summer came to an end, and we were only a few days from returning to classes. Dad called Fred and me to the table. He laid down two small piles of bills and change. "This is the money you boys paid me for room and board," he said.

We stared at the money. It was more than I had realized.

He handed it to us. "This is your money. Now let this be a lesson: Don't spend all your money just because you have it to spend. You save it. Always put something back." He smiled at us. "Did you miss out on anything important this summer because you didn't have money?"

"No," I admitted and so did Fred.

"Then I hope you've learned a lesson."

We did learn. I still live by the principle of giving God money off the top—our tithe and offerings. Then I invest some and live on the rest. It has worked well for me, and it's worked well for my siblings.

The twins reminded me years later that when they began to go out and work, Dad did the same thing to them—insisted that they pay him half of their money for room and board. They were just as excited as Fred and I had been when Dad gave it all back in August.

As I was to learn, Dad was a great budgeter and savvy spender. When we were kids and saw the amount of money Mom spent for groceries, we thought she paid out a lot. When we were a little older and realized how much it took to keep all of us fed, clothed, and out of debt, we realized we had a very wise mom and wondered how she did it on so little.

There was another thing I didn't realize until after I was in college: Mom never spent money on herself; it was always on us. When I did the washing, I noticed her underwear was sometimes old and torn, but as long as she could keep on wearing it, she didn't buy anything new. I think I was too young and too self-centered to realize why she didn't have newer clothes.

It's amazing when I think about all that they accomplished with nine kids. I just have two, and knowing how hard that was, it just blows my mind.

I remember the summer Fred and I both wanted a new bicycle, but we also knew we wouldn't have enough money to buy two of them. We wanted a special kind of bike—one only Sears made and sold—because they were especially designed to coast long distances. We were so excited about the bikes that we convinced Dad to take us to the Sears store to check them out.

Dad was also impressed, and it was obvious he wasn't just trying to make us feel good. "There's one problem, boys," he said. "They cost a lot of money."

"If we work hard and cut grass all summer, can we get one?" I asked.

"We'll both work and save all our money," Fred added.

Dad agreed but said, "They're expensive. I can't help you pay for them. So don't count on anything from me."

"We won't," I said. Fred and I were so enthusiastic, Dad agreed we could save our money for one bicycle. We had it all planned—and figured out how many lawns we would have to cut during the summer.

Fred and I followed through and worked even harder than we had originally promised. Dad watched and applauded. Before the end of the summer we had saved enough to buy the bicycle. We were so elated to have our own bike that we didn't care that we'd have to share it.

Dad went to Sears to pick it up for us. When he came home, he had two bicycles in the car.

"Two of them?" Fred asked, stunned by the sight.

Before I could add anything, Dad grinned. He handed one to each of us. "When you work hard, good things happen."

Standing there beside my brother, staring at two new bicycles—it was one of the happiest moments of my childhood.

I'm sorry to admit it, but I was a little careless with my bike.

"Be careful there," Dad said several times. "You watch out or you will break that bike."

"I'm being careful enough," I said. I guess I was so happy to have the bike, I didn't think about anything bad happening to it.

"No, you're not," Dad said. When I started to protest, his voice grew quiet and firm. "I'll give you two weeks before that bike will be broken."

"Uh-uh, Dad, I'm going to take care of it. This is a nice bike, and I won't let anything happen to it."

On the last day of the two weeks, I was racing down a hill with some of my friends. One of them swerved in front of me. I ran into him and bent my front wheel.

Shamefaced, I went home and told Dad.

"Yeah, I told you so," he said.

"I'm sorry, Dad. I should have been more careful." I assumed that by showing contrition I'd get him to buy me a new wheel or have that one repaired. He must have read my mind.

"I'm not going to get your bike fixed. If you want it fixed, you have to pay for it yourself."

"It wasn't my fault." I explained again what happened.

"You shouldn't have been racing."

I was disappointed, but Dad was right again. He knew me too well. I did save my money, and before the summer was over I had enough to get it fixed.

You can be sure I was more careful with my bike after that.

When I started my clinic, I spoke with an accountant. He said I needed to borrow thirty thousand dollars because it was a new practice; I'd have a lot of overhead for at least two months before the income made a difference.

I went to a bank for a loan. "What collateral do you have?" the manager asked.

"My M.D.," I said. "Besides, I'm from Fayetteville and I'm now a physician, and I'm not going anywhere." I explained my business plan.

He refused to give me a loan.

The refusal shocked me, but I determined not to let it show.

Bertie and I had saved money and made the down payment on a small house. It hadn't occurred to me that I'd have trouble getting a loan for the clinic. It was especially sad because I personally knew White people who had gone to the same bank with no more collateral than I had and received loans, most of them larger than the amount I wanted. I probably should have gone to another bank, and I don't know why I didn't.

When I told the family, Dad came to the rescue. "I'll mortgage my house to use as collateral," he said. There was no question with him that I'd pay the money back. "I'm not worried," he said. "I know you're going to do what you say you're going to do."

With Dad's help, I was able to secure the loan, which was for two years. Once I had the money, I said to the man, who was also an African American, "I've taken care of this, but I want to tell you something. When I get on my feet, you people will want to do further business with me. I want you to know that this is the only time you will ever get my business."

As soon as I opened my clinic, I did well. I repaid the loan in less than two years.

Later, when Fred got out of the service, Dad again put up his house as collateral for Fred's practice. I also put up property to help him secure his loan.

Neither Dad nor I had any questions about Fred's repaying the money. He was not only my brother; he was also my best friend.

From the first time any of us earned money, we learned the meaning of the tithe. We always gave a percentage of everything to the church. It wasn't even an issue; we accepted this, and it never became a problem.

Only one time did I not pay my tithe. I had been cutting grass, and the only money I had left after buying clothes was my tithe. Mom ran short of money and needed a dollar.

She knew I had money and said, "I'd like to borrow it."

"Mom, that's my tithe."

"Don't worry, son. I'll pay it back."

I handed her a dollar bill. Of course she repaid me. But I've been able to tease her through the years about the only time I couldn't pay my tithe because my mother took my money.

While we were growing up, my dad said, "If you borrow money from somebody, you pay that person back. If you don't, it's stealing." I have borrowed a few times, but I've never had any trouble paying it back. Why should I? When I asked for it, I knew I'd give it back.

I was a Harris. And this meant I handled money, like everything else, with integrity.

Chapter 14

You See God's Model for Mates

Follow God's commands for purity.

Mom loves to tell a story about Fred just before he got married during his second year at college. One of her friends said that several women at church were standing around talking and someone mentioned Fred's engagement.

"Why did he do that?" one woman asked. "Was the girl pregnant?"

"She was not," said a second woman.

"Really? How do you know?" asked the friend.

"Because I know Fred. He isn't like that." The woman who defended my brother was one of his former girlfriends.

When Mom told us, she said, "See, if you live right, people know, because your reputation follows you."

None of us did much dating in high school, even though we could have. Our parents didn't encourage it. From time to time Mom said to Fred and me, "Girls and books don't mix. You're either going to do one or the other."

Fred talked to girls more than I did. Maybe I was just shy, but I think it was because I was so focused on my studies. I didn't have much of a social life, and I didn't go to parties. I wasn't against them, and I didn't feel awkward. I just didn't have much interest.

I didn't have money to take girls out anyway, and Mom commented, "No romance without finance."

Another thing that stopped me was the way some of the students got into trouble with pregnancies and diseases. I didn't want any of that. I liked a couple of girls, but I just never asked any of them out. In fact, I never talked seriously to any girl when I was in high school.

In the back of my mind was always the thought, I'm a Harris. I don't do things just because my friends do them.

All of us still talk about the dragon meetings. We started them when Deborah was old enough to think about going out with boys, and we continued them for Mabel, Freda, and Ruth when they became teenagers.

Every time a new boy came around, Dad called a dragon meeting. The meetings worked like this: Dad and all of us boys gathered together around the kitchen table. For some reason, we boys took coat hangers, twisted them around our heads, and bent them to look like horns. We also filled bowls with Cheerios, Rice Krispies, or Corn Flakes to eat while we talked. Then we called Deborah in, and she sat down. We discussed her boyfriends and what kind of things Deborah should and shouldn't do.

We liked to think that we were offering her our wisdom and guidance. If a boy asked her out for a date, we discussed what we knew about that boy. We asked questions such as "Where are you planning to go?" "What will you do?" "What time are you coming back?"

From the boys' point of view, this was hilarious fun. We actually spied on the girls and had all kinds of techniques for watching them. The girls had no say in our decisions. We grew up in the culture where men took care of the women in their families. We believed we were merely exercising our duty to protect them.

We wanted to be sure that the boys were good enough for our sisters to date. This may sound a little chauvinistic to people today, but in the late 1960s we felt this was our responsibility.

The only difference is that if we were teens today, Dad would probably have insisted that the boys go through the same torture. We still hold those meetings today with our nephews and nieces.

I think I coined the term dragon meetings. At the time the Ku Klux Klan received a lot of publicity, and they called their leader the grand dragon. As I think back, I realize it was my way of trying to laugh at a terrible situation that went on in the South.

I now confess to my siblings that I was really worse with Deborah than with the others. When she was in high school, she met a Christian boy who also attended the church, and he was in the army, stationed at Fort Bragg. I was against him for just one reason: He rode a motorcycle, and Deborah rode on the back of it. *That's dangerous,* I rationalized. Perhaps I sound like a mother, but I worried about her. Every time I saw her on his bike, I was afraid that she'd fall off or that there would be an accident.

By the summer of 1972, between my junior and senior years at Yale, Deborah became concerned about my love life. She decided that I needed to meet a nice girl from the church she went to while attending Bennett College.

Because she kept urging me to start dating, just before I was to return to Yale for my senior year I went to visit her at Greensboro.

I had only been on the campus a few minutes when I saw a young woman walking across the street. She and Deborah waved at each other.

"Who is she?" I asked.

"Oh, that's Bertie Mitchell. She's my campus little sister."

"I want to meet her."

"She's not the girl I wanted you to meet."

"I want to meet Bertie."

I think Deborah was surprised because I had been so reluctant before. She called Bertie over and introduced us. I can tell you only that I liked Bertie the instant I first talked to her. *She is the one,* I mumbled to myself, *she will be my wife.*

Bertie was shy, and I later learned she had never dated or had a boyfriend. I've always considered that a God-sent blessing. Besides, I was too shy to strike up a conversation with a girl on my own, so if Deborah hadn't introduced us, I never would have talked to her.

Bertie and I went roller-skating that night and talked a little—it was mostly light, casual conversation. Because we skated the couples' skate dances, I held her hand while we moved around the rink. In some ways, I suppose I felt like any boy on his first date. *She's the one,* I kept thinking.

Later I told Deborah how much I liked Bertie, and I felt as if I babbled like a fifteen-year-old. Then I told her all the things I did wrong. "I guess I lost my composure. I even drove the wrong way on a one-way street."

Deborah laughed, but she agreed: Bertie must be special. I was the shy, quiet brother, and now I talked excitedly about a girl. That had never happened before.

When I left Bertie that weekend, I asked, "May I have your phone number?"

She shook her head. She never gave a reason, just a refusal. I wondered if it had been my bad driving or if she just didn't like me. Instead of getting discouraged, I determined to get to know her better. As soon as I returned to Yale I wrote her a letter. She answered, and we exchanged a few letters. At the time, I didn't know if I was in love; I did know I couldn't get Bertie Mitchell out of my mind.

When I finally found a reason to go back to Greensboro and visit Deborah again, I saw Bertie, of course. One of the first questions I asked was, "May I have your phone number so I can call you?" We had corresponded, so I thought this time it would be all right.

She shook her head. "I'm just not ready to get serious," she said.

I smiled and answered, "Okay." I decided I'd wear her down, because I knew I liked her. I talked about her all the time. Whenever I called home, Bertie was the main thing on my mind. At first, I wasn't aware that I spoke about her so much, but my siblings were. They teased me a lot.

"Is that Brother Larry who is getting excited about a girl?" asked Mitchell. My mom and dad couldn't believe it. Fred said I was "hooked."

I didn't mind the teasing, because by then I knew I had fallen in love. I knew even then that she was God-sent. Bertie and I wrote each other regularly, and we dated as much as we could under the circumstances.

On top of her being beautiful and bright, Bertie was also an excellent student. She had been valedictorian of her high school class. Yes, she was my kind of girl. As we talked, I realized that she felt as strongly about getting an education as I did.

I almost lost her one time. I had started medical school at Duke University, and I went to see her on Easter weekend. I had saved and bought new clothes, and I thought I was looking really good.

On that Sabbath at church she complimented my brother: "You look nice, Mitchell." She didn't say anything about me, and I had worn a new outfit. That not only hurt my feelings, but it also made me think she didn't like me very much.

I had planned to take her out that weekend and assumed she wouldn't hesitate. After all, I had come a long way just to see her. "Are you ready to go?" I asked. Maybe I sounded as if I were taking her for granted.

"No, I'm not going to go. I have to study."

Her words shocked me badly. I stood in front of her, not knowing what to say. I reminded myself that Bertie was a bookworm like I was.

After a lengthy silence, I said, "Uh, well, I'll just go on back to Duke." I was actually quite upset. I had driven fifty miles and bought a new outfit, and she turned me down. I decided to try to patch things up, so I dialed the pay phone in her dorm; it was busy. I headed back to Durham feeling rejected.

What I didn't know, and only later did she tell me, was that as soon as I said I was going back to school, she rushed back to her room. She was really upset. She decided that if I had really wanted to go out with her, I would have protested or at least have asked her a second time. She thought I was showing an interest in her only because of Deborah. She was so miserable and disappointed that she tore up my picture and threw it into the wastebasket. "I'll never see him again," she promised herself.

I felt miserable when I arrived back at Duke. I had planned the trip for weeks. That evening, I wrote Bertie a letter and expressed my disappointment.

She didn't answer that letter or the next two I sent her. She made it clear that she wasn't interested. In fact, almost a year passed before we actually spoke to each other. I decided to visit Greensboro. After all, I reasoned, I wanted to see my sister. I knew the real reason for my visit—and so did Deborah. I just couldn't get Bertie out of my mind. The visit was cordial, but Bertie and I spoke only when our paths crossed.

The following Easter I sent Bertie a lily. She began to talk to me again.

For the next three years, I visited, wrote, and did everything I could to change Bertie's mind about dating me. Eventually she did give me her phone number, so I called when I could afford to.

Over the next four years we grew closer, and finally Bertie did get serious. I proposed and she accepted. During my last semester of medical school, on December 19, 1976, we were married.

Our parents had talked to us about sex. My mother used to say to the girls, "If you let yourselves go and have sex before marriage, the time will come when you'll want to be with a boy, and he's not going to want you because somebody has already had you."

Dad used to say to us boys, "You need to keep yourself pure. You treat girls just the way you want a boy to treat your sister."

Both of them stressed celibacy until marriage. I was a twenty-six-year-old virgin when I married Bertie. I have been with only one woman in my whole life. I thought everyone—at least those who came from Christian homes—would be like us.

I was a bit surprised when I realized many young men didn't believe the way I did. For example, when I was in medical school, before I married Bertie, I signed up for an elective psychiatric rotation. One of the patients we discussed was a twenty-one-year-old male. He was having severe emotional problems.

Among other things the patient mentioned that he was still a virgin. A surprised expression passed quickly across the psychiatrist's face. "That's really unusual for this age," he said.

It wasn't the words he said but the way he said them. His tone implied that the man must have serious problems because he was still a virgin.

That attitude confused me, and I kept thinking about that remark. At first I thought, *Maybe I'm just messed up.* I was older than the twenty-one-year-old man, and I had never had sex.

For several days I pondered that incident. I prayed and asked for guidance. I knew the Bible taught that sexual relationships were to be reserved for those who were married. I also thought about the teachings I had received at home. My parents had stressed abstinence, but I wanted to understand the reason behind it.

My parents said not only that it was morally wrong and against the commands of the Bible, but if we had sex outside of marriage, we could easily become diseased. Even worse, we might get a girl pregnant, and that could ruin our plans for a career. That wasn't what we needed at that age.

I pondered the matter for another day or two, but I knew I had done the right thing by not playing around with girls, regardless of what others did or how the psychiatrist felt.

There certainly is a need for not only Black families but all families—especially Christians—to get back to basic family values of love, hard work, and God. Wouldn't it be great if our teenagers could be proud of the fact that they are virgins? I hope and pray that my wife and I can pass on to our children what my parents passed on to all nine of us.

I can't remember having any problems with peer pressure over sex. In our friendships outside the family, I never compromised my ideals to befriend someone. I don't think my siblings did either. I'd think of my mom reminding us, "A good name is always to be chosen, and it's better than all the riches in the world." She also used to say to me when I became friendly with other kids, "Just remember, you have to respect yourself and respect your reputation, and if you develop a bad reputation from the things you do or the things you say, then you'll pay for it in the long run. Others are always watching you." Mom also said, "You never know how your negative or positive behavior may influence others."

Even today people who knew us as kids still compliment our family on how well we behaved. In our community—so we learned—neighbors and friends considered us the model family. Every time my mother hears such words, she thanks the Lord for allowing her and my dad to teach us to live right. I consider that the most powerful legacy our family could leave the community.

197

They instilled in us that our true character is revealed in what we do when no one seems to be watching. They remind us that people compliment character as well as talent, and purity was part of our character.

We Harrises wanted to earn credit for both, and our passion for purity started at home.

Chapter 15

Family Shows You How Much You Matter

You're as good as anybody else. No one is inferior.

Our parents didn't crusade against racial prejudice or injustice. We were a patriotic family who obeyed the laws, even when they were unjust. Mom wanted me to understand something even more important than a matter of race. She wanted me to understand that I was worthwhile and equal to anyone, even if everybody couldn't accept me that way.

I'm writing this as a Black man, but it's not really just an ethnic issue. Prejudice is everywhere, and we're constantly being taught, often subliminally, that some people are superior—smarter, taller, prettier, brighter—and that means the rest must be inferior.

I don't believe that. Neither did my parents.

The day I sat on the stool at Kresge's was also the day I became aware of the drinking fountain marked "For Whites Only" and the other marked "Colored." Not only did Blacks have to sit in the back of buses or the last cars on trains, but we couldn't even sit in the same waiting room as Whites. To buy our tickets, we had to go around to the side of the building where we'd find a window. If it was raining, that didn't matter; we stayed out there even if the waiting room was empty. We couldn't go inside a restaurant; we had to go to the back, and they'd sell us something there. Of course, there was no place for us to sit and eat it, either. When traveling, we couldn't use the rest rooms, because they were only for Whites. When we went on vacation, Mom spent most of the night before cooking and preparing food for the family. No motels accepted Black customers.

When we were sick, we could see a White doctor. No matter how severe our illness, however, the doctor would look at us only after he had finished with his White patients. We had to wait outside or in a special waiting room away from the preferred patients. We faced the same situation if we went to a store to buy shoes or clothes—clerks served us at the back door.

Segregation laws caused many Blacks to feel inferior, but our parents wouldn't let us accept that. "You're as good as anybody else," both of them said to us many times.

"If you know that, it doesn't matter if other people are ignorant," Mom said once. "Just don't you ever forget."

Despite the segregation they had grown up with, Mom and Dad taught the equality of all races. They wanted their children to grow up as free from hatred and prejudice as possible. "Don't let them bring you down to their level and make prejudice a part of you." I must have heard my mother say that a dozen times. "Just get along with them and treat them nice. It's their problem and not yours."

I never saw either of my parents do anything to indicate any prejudice. They saw it around them. They knew that sometimes people discriminated against us, but they never spoke against White people. "They just don't understand" was the strongest statement I ever heard from either parent. That's amazing, because I knew prejudice hurt them.

When we lived in Germany, in military housing among other American soldiers, some of the kids got angry at us, yelled, taunted us, and called us niggers. That was a word we didn't use in our house.

One day I ran home because of the things the White kids had said. Actually, I had caused the problem. (Sometimes I stirred up trouble, and then I ran home when the kids got mad.) On that particular day, Fred and I both screamed for Mama as we outran the boys.

"Mama! Mama!" I said breathlessly as I slammed the door behind me.

"What's wrong, boys?" Mama asked.

"Those boys—they called Fred and me 'dirty niggers.'"

She held out her arms and embraced us. "Now don't you worry about that. Because anybody can be a nigger—anybody can be low-down, mean, and carnal. Being Black doesn't make you a nigger."

As she held us, I understood something. People could call me any names they wanted, and it would hurt only if I allowed it to. "They're just ignorant," Mom had said many times. "They just don't know any better."

Through the years, if I start to get upset when someone shows obvious prejudice against me, I remember Mom's words. That calms me.

Being in the apartment complex meant we lived with people from all over the United States. We encountered prejudice, and I'm not sure it was always racial. Our family was different, and that often is enough reason for prejudice.

We were unlike those around us in several ways. For one thing, my mother cooked differently from most of the people we knew. Our church taught people healthy living and to care for their bodies. We ate a limited amount of meat, and Mom refused to buy any pork products. The other kids laughed at us because we wouldn't eat hot dogs and bacon.

"What's wrong with hot dogs?" they asked.

"They're just not good for you" was the best I could answer. That brought more laughs.

We were also the largest family in the complex, and we frequently heard snide remarks. Sometimes adults said unkind things right in our presence. "Maybe someone needs to learn the facts of life," one woman said. Because she smiled, we were supposed to think it was funny.

I don't think we smiled, and we sure didn't laugh; however, our parents didn't allow us to be rude.

Mom said many times, "If you treat them mean back, you're no better than they are. You be nice, no matter how mean they are to you."

Mom and Dad not only taught that principle, but they lived the example for us to follow.

Following our parents' example wasn't always easy, especially in the face of prejudice. When I started school in North Carolina, my first-grade teacher was a light-skinned Black. I remember her vividly because of the negative ways she spoke about our race.

"White children know how to behave," she said frequently. If one of us in our all-Black class did something she didn't like, she quickly said, "White children don't misbehave the way you do." She kept trying to change us to imitate not just mannerly behavior, but White people.

When a White man from the superintendent's office came to visit our school one day, the teacher saw him from the window and told us, "Stand up, everyone! Look at that White gentleman."

Obediently, we got out of our seats, went to the window, and stared.

"See how he walks?" the teacher said. "Notice that he's walking straight. That's the way to do it, and you children don't walk like that."

Even though I was only six years old, it hurt me to hear her talk that way. My parents had stressed that color didn't make one person better than another.

"You're just as good as anybody else," Mom said when I asked her after one of my teacher's daily lectures. "White kids and Black kids aren't really much different. White kids misbehave just like Black kids."

As I think about it, I realize Mom didn't want to speak against my teacher, and she wouldn't allow us to do so. Yet she wouldn't let racial prejudice—even from a Black woman—go unchallenged.

Mom told me, "You have to understand that she just doesn't understand. It's not really her fault. That's the way she was trained. Someone messed with her mind to make her think she's not as good as Whites and to believe that anything Black is bad or inferior."

Her final words to me were "I'll take care of it." I knew that Mom wouldn't let my teacher continue to talk that way.

I have no idea how many trips she made to that teacher's room to talk to her or the principal.

I do know our teacher stopped talking about how Whites were better. I never forgot her, and I sometimes wonder how many children in her classes allowed that kind of prejudice to beat them down. All of them didn't have great parents like ours who kept reminding us that we were as good as anyone else.

I encountered less obvious prejudice as well, even as early as first grade. That same year, there was a girl in our class who was the daughter of another teacher. Because the girl could read well, the school administrators pulled her out of our class and promoted her to second grade.

That really upset me. Yes, she read well, but not any better than I did. I was crying by the time I got home, because I felt that I was being overlooked. I told my mother, "I can read just as well as she can—why can't I go? I think it's just because my mom's not a teacher and hers is."

"We'll find out about what's going on," my mother said. My mother went to the school and talked to the teacher about the promotion. Even though my teacher admitted I was as good a reader as the girl, the principal shrugged. "That's just the way it is."

Mom, smart enough to realize that getting angry wouldn't help, got up to leave. She turned to me, hugged me, and said, "Larry, you just go on doing what you're doing. You're smart and you read well. It doesn't matter what anyone else says. You just keep trying your best."

I didn't get promoted, but Mom made me feel so good that it was all right.

My fifth-grade teacher was an older White woman whom I adored. Why not? I was the smartest kid in the class. I made all A's (except in penmanship), and she frequently praised me for my work. I had only one problem in her class.

"I'm going to take you off the honor roll, Larry," she said several times, "if you don't improve your handwriting."

"Yes, ma'am," I said.

"You write just like a doctor."

Isn't it interesting that I never forgot that statement? Perhaps it has stayed with me because, even then, I think I already knew what I wanted to do with my life.

The next year, when I was in sixth grade, I was still the smartest student. My teacher, a young White woman, however, was prejudiced, and she gave me a B or a C whenever she could. She used to read us stories such as Joel Chandler Harris's tales of Brer Rabbit, and once she really insulted us by reading the story *Little Black Sambo*. Never mind that out of a class of thirty, four of us were Black.

One other thing I recall about my sixth-grade teacher was that she pronounced the word *Negro* as "Niggra." The fact that she even talked about the difference irritated me, but I just kept doing my best. I didn't say much—I was learning to just drive on.

The worst thing about that sixth-grade teacher was that she wouldn't give me straight A's when I had earned them.

In the middle of the year, my fifth-grade teacher asked how I was doing. She was shocked to hear I wasn't still earning A's and confronted the sixth-grade teacher. "This boy is very smart," she said. "He was the smartest child I had last year. I know he's trying very hard. I cannot understand why you are grading him so low."

"I don't think he's grade-A material," my sixth-grade teacher replied.

No matter what my fifth-grade teacher said, my sixth-grade teacher remained firm.

I complained to Mom about my teacher's obvious prejudice. Mom talked to her, but the woman adamantly said she had no prejudices of any kind. She still gave me grades of B and C whenever we did essay tests. I knew my work was better than most of those who received A's—and, of course, all of them were White.

Instead of getting angry, my mother told me to keep a record of all my test scores. If the teacher didn't give me the grade I earned, at least I would have the evidence to confront her.

I started recording my scores—and the teacher knew it. Immediately my grades returned to A's.

When I entered tenth grade, I went to a high school off the army base in Fayetteville. That was the same year they integrated the school system.

Then I encountered prejudice of a different kind. One of my teachers regularly belittled my faith. I don't know if it was a personal attack on me or just that she hated religion, but she didn't allow any opportunity to slip by without speaking against the Christian faith.

She referred to it as "fairy-tale religion" or made statements such as "If you want to believe that, go ahead; but then, most educated people would argue against you." I couldn't let her rave against the Christian faith day after day. At first I tried to be polite, but finally I challenged her.

The longer the class continued, the more antagonistic she became. I couldn't enjoy the class. I didn't want to go every day and end up arguing with her. Finally, I told Mom what was going on.

"I'll take care of it," Mom said.

The next day Mom was at school, and she talked to the teacher. I don't know what she said, but the teacher never belittled my faith again.

During my senior year, I heard the other students talk about who would be the valedictorian—the person with the highest grade point average. It's odd, but no one asked me if I thought I had a chance. Maybe it was because I didn't go around telling everyone what grades I received. As I listened to them talk, they threw others' names back and forth. I didn't offer any opinions.

I had had one unfair academic experience in high school. I received one B in high school, and it came from my eleventh-grade English teacher. I knew I had earned an A because I kept track carefully. I also knew I had the highest score in the class.

When I saw the B, I went into her classroom and respect-fully asked her to change my grade. I told her why and handed her my list of grades in her class.

"You received a B because you didn't participate enough in class," she said.

I knew that wasn't true, and I said so.

"Besides, I never give anyone an A the first semester."

"That's crazy reasoning. I worked hard and I deserve an A."

"That is my decision," she said and refused to yield.

Like Dad said, I drove on. I felt she had cheated me. Only momentarily did I feel discouraged that time. At the beginning of eleventh grade, I carefully recorded all the grades of the other high achievers. I knew I still stood an excellent chance of being the top student in my class. Right then I had a grade point average of 3.89 out of 4.00. No one student had anything higher.

I had no trouble knowing the academic standing of the others. At the end of each grading period, most of the students went around and shared scores with each other.

I wrote down what the bright students told me, so I knew which ones had the highest grades and what they were. I also continued to keep a record of my own grades to make sure I received fair treatment. I used that information to compete with the other top students.

That same year, the other students elected me president of the student body, as well as "Most Likely to Succeed," "Most Dependable," and "Most Versatile."

Because of my academic achievement, some of my fellow students used to call me *lame* (similar to *nerd* or *egghead* today) because I was so committed to my books. I had only one girlfriend when I was in high school, and that lasted only about two weeks. We never really went anywhere, but I liked her and she liked me. To me, that constituted having a girlfriend.

Sometimes I did feel like a nerd. But I still recall something Fred said to me. I complained, "Some of the kids think I'm lame because I don't go to parties and have girlfriends."

"No, I think you're real smart for hitting the books, and I wish I were more like you."

His words stunned me. Fred was my hero, my idol, and he wanted to be more like me? That was also about the time that Fred decided to get serious about his future and began to study harder.

A few weeks before graduation, the principal called all five of the top achievers into his office. The principal congratulated us for our work and told us how proud he was of us. "Today," he said, "I am going to announce the class valedictorian."

I looked around at the others, and I already knew where each of us stood, so I tried not to let on. Then a fearful thought struck me: I knew my grades and I knew their grades, but would I encounter some kind of prejudice again? Would the principal or one of the teachers find a way to lower some of my grades? For several minutes, the anxiety burned within me.

"The student with the highest grade-point average in the class of 1969 is Larry Coleman Harris."

I smiled, I laughed, and I think I even shouted a little. I had set my goal and I had achieved it. I had proved that I could stand up against the prejudice against me.

The one time I wasn't sure I could make it at Yale was when I had to take physics in the first semester of my second year. I've mentioned that I failed that class—but not because I didn't know the material. I failed because I was so uptight. I had prepared and studied for it, and I had planned to take the test before the Christmas holidays. Then the professor gave us the option of taking the exam before or after the holidays. Unwisely, I chose the latter. We went home for Christmas, and I forgot about classes at Yale—and that was my mistake.

When I returned after the holidays, because I hadn't studied, the material wasn't fresh. I couldn't remember some of it. Besides, I had felt so sure about the content of the test, I studied only what I thought the teacher would ask about. That was my second mistake—the instructor asked questions about material I had known before the vacation period, but I just couldn't remember everything three weeks later. If I had been more relaxed and focused, I could have passed—perhaps not with a top grade—but passed anyway.

Instead, I failed.

I was distressed—it was the first time I had ever failed any class in my entire life. To make it worse, I had done so by two points.

I had to pass physics to stay in the premed program. This wasn't a class I could just drop.

That was the worst time in my entire academic life. Briefly, I considered quitting college and going out to find a job. As I said before, first I called home.

"You can do it," my mother said. "It's not the end of the world for you, and you learned something."

If I had dropped out, my parents would have been very upset. They would have said, "You gave up too easily. You quit fighting."

Although they had never told us that we had to go to college, they had both said that whatever we decided to do, we needed to stick to it and not give up.

I felt so crushed and stupid that I wondered what I was doing at a university like Yale. The only reason I didn't give up was that I couldn't face disappointing my parents. "If you fail trying to do a good job, fine," Dad once said, "but don't fail by not trying your best."

I went in to see the professor and asked for his help.

"If you had been to any of the study sessions, I could see giving you a break, but—"

"Sir, I have not missed one session. I went to every one."

"Really? I don't recall having seen you."

That saddened me. Did he lie? Was this discrimination? I don't know, because I just couldn't believe he hadn't noticed me. I vividly recalled asking him questions on at least two occasions.

He insisted he had not seen me.

In truth, we had between two hundred and three hundred students in the class. Each study group was composed of twenty to thirty people, and the sessions were strictly voluntary. Even though voluntary, I considered the sessions requirements for me and never missed any. In my group, I wasn't the most vocal, but I participated and asked questions. I was as active as anyone else in the group.

Yet he insisted he didn't remember me. I couldn't figure that out or make sense of it except to call it prejudice.

He refused to raise my grade the needed two points to put me over the passing line. I explained how badly I needed to pass physics.

"That is not my concern," he said.

Consequently, I took the course again and from a different professor. I had no problems the second time and did extremely well. From then on, I knew I could handle anything at Yale or at any other university.

I felt almost as if I were starting high school again. I prayed and asked God to help me become the best student in my class. I worked hard, and the harder I worked, the more my grades improved. By the time I finished my first semester of my senior year, I had all A's. In the second semester I had one B and all the rest were A's.

With God's help, I had proved myself once again.

When I was in my first internship as a pediatrician, something happened that brought back memories of first grade. I was in the clinic preparing to see patients when I overheard two young Black mothers talking. "I sure hope my baby doesn't have to have a Black intern," one of them said. "I want a White doctor."

I felt devastated—my own people preferring the White residents because they thought or had been subtly taught that White was better. It reminded me of my Black first-grade teacher who told us that White children acted better than Black children.

Mitchell, who has faced his share of prejudice, particularly remembers our mother saying to us, "Hold your head up. Don't look down at the ground. You're somebody because you're a Harris."

Mitchell added, "That was very important to me, growing up in a racist society. For example, even though my father was in the service, we went to the barber shop on base and were told 'We don't cut Blacks' hair.' Or sometimes they said, 'We don't cut hair for your kind of folks here.'"

I don't think any of us fell into the prejudice trap, because our parents constantly gave us the positive message: Be proud of who you are, hold up your head, your name is Harris. By keeping your head high, people will respect you and who you are.

Mitchell reminds me that my parents had the philosophy that if we made a mistake, the important thing was to learn from that experience. They punished us when we did something wrong. When the punishment time was over, Dad would say, "Now learn from this. Pick up the pieces and drive on." He also used to say, "Keep pushing. Persistence wears down resistance."

Mitch says that he used that philosophy in school, and especially in college. When he entered the workforce in 1977 there were very few Blacks in the Southeast part of the company. Mitch realized his boss wasn't pleased to have him on the team.

> He started talking against me to some of his colleagues, and of course the word got back to me that he would be getting rid of me soon. I determined that no matter what happened I was going to drive on. The challenges of being Black in corporate America in the 1970s and '80s didn't encourage me to work my way up in the company. But I kept hearing my dad say, "Drive on," or my mom telling me, "Keep going, you're going to win." I did just that—I kept trying. I kept pushing and driving on until I made my goal of becoming a sales manager.
>
> My boss never did fire me. He moved on, but I stayed and rose in the company.

Sometimes we face prejudice and opposition, and those are the times we need to stand up. Each year we pediatricians have an annual meeting. Representatives from all the pharmaceutical companies come, pass out samples, and try to get us to prescribe their products.

At the 1990 conference, we were lined up and the representatives came up to us and handed us a gift package. One sales rep passed right by me.

"Excuse me," I said, "you didn't give me a gift. I'm a physician."

"Oh? Sorry. I didn't know you were a doctor—I, uh, didn't see you."

That was impossible. She had gone directly from the man on my right to the man on my left.

I pointed to my name tag. "See this? It reads *Dr.* in front of my name." I didn't point out that every person in the room was either a doctor or a representative of a pharmaceutical company.

"You bypassed me," I went on to say, "because I don't look like the other doctors in this room."

"That's not true," she said weakly, handed me the gift package, and moved on.

Two years later, when I attended the annual conference, a White doctor came up to me. "You don't know me, and we've never talked before, but I was standing behind you two years ago." He reminded me of the pharmaceutical sales rep. "You did the right thing," he said.

Yes, I knew I had done the right thing.

I learned that from my parents. We Harrises are as good as anyone else. Our assurance started at home.

Conclusion

Still Together

Our family has remained together in spite of troubled waters. In June 1993 the whole family attended our church's annual camp meeting. Except for my father, who decided to remain at the hotel, we all returned to the campground for evening prayer service.

When I returned from the service, I heard someone crying as if in terrible pain. At first I thought it was a teenager playing a game. When I walked into my parents' room, however, I saw Freda wailing in agony.

The head of our family, my father, Fred Harris Jr., had died. Freda had found him. He had suffered for years from Parkinson's disease.

Aside from the tremendous sorrow, I also felt guilty. Why hadn't I stayed at the hotel with my father? Maybe, as a physician, I could have revived him. Why did God allow this to happen while we were at church camp meeting? I was feeling my own grief, struggling with my own guilt, as I continually wiped tears from my eyes.

Fred and Ruth on their fortieth wedding anniversary, Fayetteville, NC, April 13, 1989

My mother, with the courage of a lion and the faith of a helpless newborn, said, "It's all right. The Lord knows best."

We survived that loss.

Eight months later, on April 23, 1994, another tragedy visited our family. I was sure that this would destroy my mother: Her first child, Fred Harris III, was killed in a private airplane crash.

I didn't want to believe it, and in some ways I had a harder time than Mom did. Fred was supposed to live forever. After all, he was my big brother, and he was responsible to look after me.

Once again, my mother's faith was unyielding. Her strength provided courage for her remaining eight children. "It's going to be all right. We'll see Fred and Freddie [her name for Dad] again in heaven." She said those words with such conviction none of us doubted that she meant them. They certainly weren't pat phrases to try to make us feel better.

Occasionally I preach at my church. In one sermon, I expressed our family sorrow this way:

> At times the storms of life may seem unconquerable. We're all faced with seemingly hopeless situations. Do you have high blood pressure? Diabetes? Cataracts? A bad heart that required open-heart bypass surgery? I have all of them. Have you lost a brother and a father in the same year? I did. Did you lose your husband to sudden death? My sister Mabel did. Is your child on crack cocaine or in jail? I know families like that. What are your problems? Are you about to lose your job? Your home?
>
> God doesn't exempt any of us from trials and tribulations. As long as we live on this earth, we're going to face sadness and heartache. We're going to encounter sickness and loss of loved ones.
>
> Should we complain about going through so many life storms on this earth? No! We shouldn't complain, because going through them is better than being stuck in the mud of the greater disaster of sin.

There is no doubt that my mother lived this and taught us to live it too. She has said many times, "Accept what God has allowed." Her attitude echoes the words of a gospel song that says, "Nobody told us that the way would be easy."

I concluded my sermon by saying, "We must have faith to trust in a God who loves us. We must believe that the storms of life cause our physical and spiritual electricity to fail, but God remains the generator that turns the power back on."

When Fred was gone, I became the big brother in the family.

I want to be as good an older brother as he was. I probably won't, but I'll always be thankful for him. He loved me, he taught me, and he set an example for me.

The final thing I want to say—and this would be true of all of us—is this: Whatever we've amounted to in this life, it's because our parents wisely and lovingly put family first and taught us the right way to go. All of our success started at home.

The Principles

Ways to Keep the Family First

1. Honor your name—it is the most important thing you have.
2. When you live what you teach, your family has no trouble following.
3. God is premier, and then the family.
4. Stand together and stand up for each other.
5. Each child is responsible for the next younger child.
6. Your best friends are your family members.
7. Always be willing to give to those less fortunate.
8. Respect each other and respect those older.
9. Don't compromise to be recognized. You'll be recognized because you don't compromise.
10. Any honest job is good.
11. Set goals and achieve them.
12. In the face of failure and disappointment, drive on.
13. Pay back what you borrow or it's stealing.
14. Follow God's commands for purity.
15. You're as good as anybody else. No one is inferior.

Fred and Ruth Harris proudly seated at the center in the last family portrait, taken in 1988, with all members alive. Standing, left to right: Deborah, Larry, Fred III (deceased 1994), Dyfierd, Mitchell, Michael, and Mabel. Seated, left to right: Ruth, Dad (deceased 1993), Mom, and Freda.

Larry C. Harris, M.D., is a graduate of Yale University and Duke University Medical School. He runs a private pediatric practice in Fayetteville, North Carolina, where he lives with his wife, Bertie, and their two children.

Cecil ("Cec") Murphey is an award-winning author or co-author of more than ninety books, including *The Relentless God.* He cowrote *Gifted Hands* with Dr. Ben Carson and *Rebel with a Cause,* Franklin Graham's autobiography.